Only four days after his inauguration, President Kennedy issued an executive order creating a White House Food for Peace Office and appointed Senator George McGovern, Democrat from South Dakota, its first Director. The speed with which this action was taken is dramatic evidence of the importance which the Administration attaches to the international food problem.

"It has taken the entire history of the human race," writes Senator McGovern in *War Against Want*, "to bring the population of the planet to its present level of three billion people. Yet the best projections indicate that by the year 2000, another three billion people will have been added to the world population . . . Our present annual food production would not meet the needs of a world population of six billion for a fortnight."

How to feed the starving multitudes of this world has long since ceased to be the exclusive concern of theoretical economists and generous humanitarians. It has come to be a gigantic global nightmare which directly affects the conscience and the security of every person on the planet.

in the underdeveloped world."

War Against Want is a discussion of this awesome subject by the American perhaps best qualified to write about it. Senator McGovern lucidly describes the dimensions of the problem, what has been done to deal with it, and what is being planned. He draws on his extensive eyewitness experience to present his urgent message in vividly and often shockingly human terms. As President Johnson indicates in his foreword, the message of *War Against Want* is one of vital importance for every American.

WAR AGAINST WANT

WAR AGAINST WANT:

America's Food for Peace Program

SENATOR GEORGE S. McGOVERN

Foreword by

PRESIDENT LYNDON B. JOHNSON

WALKER AND COMPANY

New York

Dedicated to
MY MOTHER
and the memory of
MY FATHER

Foreword

HUNGER—mankind's most persistent enemy—can be conquered. Half the people on earth need no longer face a future without enough food. With present skills and resources we can grow enough food to provide every man, woman, and child an adequate diet.

Our challenge, then, is to find ways to meet the food needs of the developing nations through the increasingly bountiful harvests of the advanced nations—and to provide a fair return to the producer for his labors.

For ten years America has pioneered in such an effort. Public Law 480, the Agricultural Trade Development and Assistance Act of 1954, has provided the machinery to share our agricultural abundance with starving millions.

President John F. Kennedy knew that we have a moral duty to use our abundance to feed the hungry. His first Executive Order released Government food stocks to needy West Virginians. His second created the first full-time Food for Peace Office in The White

House. And he instructed its first Director, the author of this book, to use the nation's prosperity to "narrow the gap between abundance here at home and near starvation abroad."

We *have* narrowed that gap. Today the Food for Peace program is a shining example of human compassion. It is more than a monument to a high moral purpose—it is a living legacy of practical economic wisdom. Besides meeting the most elementary human need, our food resources are being used around the world to build schools, dig irrigation ditches, pay U.S. bills abroad, and create new markets for American agriculture.

I can personally testify to the great good this program is doing. In distant parts of the world I have seen it bring strength to replace weakness and hope to replace despair.

Seneca once observed that "a hungry people listens not to reason, nor cares for justice. . . ." The free institutions we value so highly cannot flourish where men are prisoners of need. Food for Peace, the Peace Corps, and our other overseas programs confirm our national resolve to advance the cause of freedom and human dignity by every peaceful means.

The story of Food for Peace is told well in this book by a man who knows the story intimately. In addition to his service as the first Food for Peace Director, George McGovern has served on the Agriculture Committees of both the House of Representatives and the United States Senate. It is a tribute both to his knowl-

edge of agriculture and to his legislative skill that he
was chosen, while still a freshman Senator, to guide
the 1964 Farm Bill safely through the Senate. As a
South Dakotan, he knows the problems and the achieve-
ments of the true hero of the Food for Peace program—
the American farmer.

This book is an encouraging record of American
concern and a call for action to complete the job of
building a great world society free from hunger and
hate.

Lyndon B. Johnson

June 19, 1964

Prologue

DURING the Presidential campaign of 1960, I introduced Senator John F. Kennedy to fifty thousand farmers who stood in a chilling drizzle to hear his views on agriculture at the site of the National Plowing Contest near Sioux Falls, South Dakota.

Although Mr. Kennedy spoke of farm price supports and supply management with his usual eloquence and urgency, I felt that he was not at ease with the prepared manuscript, and the crowd reacted indifferently.

Two hours later, he walked onto the stage of the Corn Palace at Mitchell, South Dakota, my home town, where a jam-packed crowd had been waiting for two hours. This time, without a note, he spoke in terms that deeply moved his listeners.

"I don't regard the...agricultural surplus as a problem," he said. "I regard it as an opportunity... not only for our own people, but for people all around the world."

"Fellow Americans facing a difficult future," Mr. Kennedy said, "I think the farmers can bring more credit, more lasting goodwill, more chance for freedom, more chance for peace, than almost any other group of Americans in the next ten years, if we recognize that food is strength, and food is peace, and food is freedom, and food is a helping hand to people around the world whose goodwill and friendship we want."

A few weeks later the 1960 campaign ended with John Kennedy the winner by a narrow margin. His own victory had scarcely been confirmed when he telephoned me from his father's home in Palm Beach to express regret over my defeat in a race for the U.S. Senate. He suggested that I talk with him after he returned to Washington before making any plans. On December 16 he asked me to serve as director of a newly proposed White House Office of Food for Peace to strengthen the use of our agricultural surpluses as a constructive instrument of American foreign policy.

The paradox of agricultural surpluses in a world of hungry people had long been a major concern of mine. During four years as a member of the House of Representatives, I had spoken out on the need to use our food abundance to feed the hungry abroad and had urged the creation of an executive office for this purpose.

Neither the President nor I had a fully defined view as to what such an office would encompass or how it could best be established. Indeed, there was a period of uncertainty as to where the office should be located and how I would secure a staff without Congressional action or a budget.

I resolved the first of these problems by moving into a vacant suite of rooms in the old Executive Office Building next to the White House and claiming them for a Food for Peace staff that I hoped to assemble in some fashion as yet unknown.

In the opening hours of his administration, on January 24, 1961, the President issued an Executive Order creating the Office of Food for Peace. He instructed me as the first Director to exercise "affirmative leadership and continuous supervision over the various activities" involved in our overseas food programs. He called upon me "to consider very carefully the intimate relationships between our foreign agricultural activities and other aspects of our foreign assistance program."

In an accompanying memorandum to the heads of government departments and agencies, Mr. Kennedy said:

"American agricultural abundance offers a great opportunity for the United States to promote the interests of peace in a significant way and to play an important role in helping to provide a more adequate diet for peoples all around the world. We must make the most vigorous and constructive use possible of this opportunity. We must narrow the gap between abundance here at home and near starvation abroad. Humanity and prudence, alike, counsel a major effort on our part."

The President's Food for Peace action of January 24

was the second Executive Order of his administration. His first order called for a stepped-up food distribution program for needy Americans. The President had been deeply moved during his primary election campaign in West Virginia by the plight of the people in the distressed mining areas of that State. He was appalled by the meager food ration the unemployed families were receiving.

His first Executive Order demonstrated continuing concern for the yearning faces he remembered in West Virginia. It was characteristic of Mr. Kennedy that he moved to secure a more adequate diet for his needy countrymen before stepping up food assistance abroad.

For various reasons the overseas food efforts of the United States during the previous decade were not very well known. Heretofore, those efforts were regarded largely as temporary "surplus disposal" operations. It was almost as though the needy countries of the world were doing us a favor by letting us give away or sell under concessional arrangements our unwanted farm surpluses.

My top assistants, James W. Symington and Nelson Post, and I decided, therefore, that a vital function of our office would be to help give a new face as well as a more dynamic force to the use of American farm surpluses overseas. Our staff of half a dozen assistants borrowed from other government agencies worked hard to dramatize America's food abundance as a tool for peace and freedom. We sought to give the farmer and the taxpayer a feeling of prideful participation in the success of U.S. foreign policy.

We pressed especially hard two appealing aspects— the overseas school lunch program and the use of food as a tool of economic and social development, including food payments to workers engaged in community development projects. These continue as two of the most hopeful opportunities of Food for Peace, now under the able direction of Mr. Richard Reuter.

President Lyndon B. Johnson reaffirmed his long-time support for Food for Peace in his first State of the Union Message when he called for "increased use of our food as an instrument of peace." In a later message to Congress, President Johnson described Food for Peace as "a powerful instrument of our foreign policy— directed toward peace, progress, freedom, and human dignity."

I shall always be grateful to President Kennedy and my fellow citizens for permitting me to serve for eighteen months in this inspiring program. This experience has given me a growing realization of the urgent demands of one of the world's great paradoxes—abundance in a world of want.

It has also strengthened my conviction that the amazing productivity of our farmers is America's most valuable material resource in today's world and even more surely in the world of tomorrow.

Four out of five inhabitants of the planet live in rural areas. Most of them are clinging to life by means of primitive farming techniques little changed since the days of Moses. The overwhelming majority are hungry. Some of them may have heard reports that the space age is here and that men who have orbited the earth are now reaching for the moon. But they are more interested in staying alive on earth than traveling to the moon.

The man who can show them how to put more food on their tables looms as a far greater hero than an astronaut. No one understands this better than the Communist leaders; yet it is in the field of agriculture where Communism has suffered its most conspicuous failures. The Soviets have matched us in outer space, but they have fallen down on the farm. Russia and China have devoted a vastly higher percentage of their manpower to agriculture than we; yet, they have been forced to import large quantities of grain while we concentrate on managing our abundance.

America's rural heartland—once the cradle of isolationism—is now a dynamic force in American foreign policy. The American farmer is the new internationalist.

This is so because our food producers need the expanding markets of a growing world and because the hungry masses of the world need our food.

And that is the story of Food for Peace—America's war against want.

Acknowledgments

I am grateful to Mr. Richard W. Reuter, my successor as Director of Food for Peace, for his careful reading of the manuscript and his helpful suggestions. Mr. James W. Symington, my former deputy, now a Washington attorney, Mr. Nelson Post, my former assistant and now an official with the Agency for International Development, and Mr. Frank Ellis, also an AID official, have read the manuscript and gave me the benefit of their thorough understanding of the Food for Peace program.

A special note of thanks is due the indomitable Mr. Theodore Granik, who provided the initial suggestion and inspiration which persuaded me to write this book.

I, of course, am responsible for any errors in fact or interpretation that may have crept into the manuscript.

—GEORGE McGOVERN

Contents

WAR AGAINST WANT

CHAPTER I

The Challenge of Hunger

"The great challenge of today is the paradox that for the first time in history we have the ability to produce enough food to feed everybody in the world. Yet, half of those people go to bed hungry each night."
—Richard W. Reuter, Director of Food for Peace,
June 25, 1963

"SHE is the symbol of the underdeveloped country," the Brazilian economist said as he saw me staring at the shapeless young mother.

I met her in a village in northeast Brazil in early 1961 on my first overseas mission as Director of the Food for Peace program.

Her face bore the unmistakable signs of under-nourishment and neglect as she sat on the mud floor of her hut. Lying with their heads on her lap were two frail children, their eyes open but without childish light. A seven-year-old brother had died the day before of smallpox aggravated by the debilitating malnutrition endemic to the area.

In subsequent months, I saw this scene duplicated countless times in the crowded slums of Hong Kong,

Rio de Janeiro, and Bombay, and in the villages and back country of India, Africa, and Latin America.

Half a billion people in today's world are chronically hungry. Another billion have poorly balanced diets. Together, they make up half of the three billion inhabitants of the globe. Lethargy, chronic illness, and early death are their companions. Their average life span is about thirty years, which someone has said is "not very long to live but a long time to be hungry." For these vast multitudes, hunger is the most important fact of life. If one doubts that, let him reduce his diet to a bowl of rice, a piece of bread, or a handful of beans for a few days and then ask himself what he most desires in life.

"Visualize a line starting from your front door, made up of the hungry of the world—many ragged and disease-ravaged, with pinched faces," wrote Donald K. Faris. "The line goes on out of sight over continent and ocean, around the world—25,000 miles—and returns to your front door. On and on it stretches, circling the globe not twice nor five times, but twenty-five, and there is no one in the line but hungry, suffering humanity."

About forty times as many of the children in these undernourished families die before reaching the age of five as in well-fed nations such as the United States. One of the basic causes of the annual death of an estimated ten million infants from intestinal and respiratory disease is a lack of proper food.

In Africa, protein deficiency takes a heavy toll among

children after weaning and before the age of six or seven. This deficiency, known as *kwashiorkor,* is recognized by the distended belly and gaunt limbs that mark the children in large areas of that continent.

Malnutrition not only restricts the physical development of children, but seriously limits their mental and emotional growth. They simply do not have the physical energy that makes education and learning possible.

In eighty-five countries of Africa, Asia, and Latin America only half of the 250,000,000 primary-age children are enrolled in schools; so, every year twenty or twenty-five million are added to the illiterate adult population, which already embraces 40 percent of the world's people.

Hunger and ignorance contribute to low economic productivity as a part of a self-perpetuating vicious circle. It is exceedingly difficult for those lacking both energy and rudimentary education to contribute much to the income or development of their nations. Most of these people live in miserable poverty on average incomes of less than $100 a year. By comparison, the U.S. average is $2,316.

Yet, it is now possible for the United States and other technically advanced nations to provide food for most of the hungry of today's world. More fundamentally, we can help them produce more food for themselves and improve their capacity to purchase additional food in regular commercial channels.

The United States is uniquely qualified to lead the campaign against world hunger. We are blessed with an agricultural technology and skilled farmers whose efficiency is the greatest single success story of the American economy. Indeed, the quiet sharing of American food and agricultural know-how may prove to have been the most helpful contribution we have made to the world since the end of World War II. But even larger challenges loom ahead in using our abundance and sharing our skills.

The productivity of the American farmer has doubled since the end of World War II. In that time the output per man-hour of our farmers has increased three times as fast as the productivity in other parts of our economy. With the percentage of Americans engaged in farming dwindling to an unprecedented 8 percent, our farms are producing more efficiently each year. Our citizens can purchase a better diet with a smaller proportion of their income than any other people of the globe. While we are spending less than one-fifth of our family income for food, the people of India are devoting more than three-fifths of their income to food; yet, the per capita daily expenditure there is only 10 cents.

We have large surpluses of wheat, feed grains, and dairy products. Vast food-producing capacity has been idled only by strenuous control efforts. Canada, Australia, Argentina, New Zealand, Burma, and Thailand also have surplus food capacity. Within a few years, Europe will be producing more food than it can consume.

One cannot imagine a more startling paradox than large food surpluses and unused agricultural capacity in a hungry, undernourished world. Yet, we live on an affluent island in a sea of poverty. While millions hunger, we struggle to meet the problem of surplus production and overeating.

We discard enough food in our disposal units and garbage cans to feed well any one of fifty nations in the underdeveloped world. We pay our farmers enough to idle surplus acreage to finance the shipment of millions of bushels of grain to the hungry abroad. We invest enough in storing and handling our surplus each year—a billion dollars—to underwrite a greatly expanded school lunch program overseas.

We live with a crisis of abundance in a world of want.

Is there an answer to this paradox? The great religions of the world would not hesitate to answer: Yes, feed the hungry.

In the words of the Koran: "An abominable sin is to sleep on a full stomach while your neighbor is sleeping on an empty stomach."

"Cast thy bread upon the waters: for thou shalt find it after many days," admonished the Hebrew prophet in Ecclesiastes.

"Inasmuch as ye have done it unto one of the least of these my brethren, ye have done it unto me," said the Teacher of Galilee.

"If thine enemy hunger, feed him," wrote St. Paul in his letter to the Romans.

Other religions of the world similarly call for the sharing of bread with those in need.

Moral considerations aside, it does seem that if man can conquer space, he should be able to provide on earth for his most rudimentary needs. Yet, those who have grappled with the task know that it is not easy to feed the hungry.

We are faced with two challenges in the war against hunger. The first is the immediate problem of sharing our present abundance to close the nutritional gap of this decade. A much more difficult challenge is to encourage and partially underwrite an agricultural revolution in the less-developed world to meet the needs of a world population that may double within thirty-five years.

Americans who look at our food surplus often wonder why we cannot simply load it into ships and send it on its way to the hungry. We have been doing that on a growing scale, but it has not been an easy task.

Our efforts to donate or sell our food under concessional terms always face difficult obstacles. We must first of all be careful not to dissipate the incentive of other people to increase their own food production in becoming overly dependent on outside assistance.

We must also protect the domestic market prices of farmers in the receiving countries by avoiding the dumping of American food into local markets.

Likewise, we must exercise caution in protecting the normal commercial market of our exporters and those of other nations.

There are other tough problems involved in giving away food. Most of the poorer countries are lacking in port facilities. In many cases, they lack experienced and reliable personnel to supervise the distribution of commodities to prevent their falling into black-market channels.

Many geographic areas where needs are greatest are without even the crudest roads and transportation facilities. These nearly inaccessible areas become even more isolated in times of flood, drought, or other calamities.

To appreciate the difficulties involved in getting food into the hands of the hungry in underdeveloped areas one need only consider the enormous investment we have made in the food industry to meet the needs of our own people. A sizable portion of American manpower and resources are devoted to the production, storage, hauling, processing, packaging, distribution, and retailing of food in the United States. This is a highly developed industry embracing millions of skilled people and billions of dollars. No such network of skills, resources, and facilities is available to handle and distribute food in any of the developing nations— even when the food is a gift.

Then, too, there is the problem of dietary habits, taboos, and religious beliefs. The "sacred cow" in India is well known. These animals, protected against slaughter by Indian religious views, eat enough grain to feed millions of hungry people. Furthermore, dietary habits have made it difficult for the Indians to accept American wheat as a substitute for the empty rice bowl. Similar dietary problems face us in other areas.

The obstacles to any successful effort to eliminate hunger and poverty in the developing nations, even at present population levels, are formidable. Those obstacles loom larger in terms of the agricultural revolution that must be effected in the next three or four decades to meet the needs of the year 2000.

The task of reconstructing the economy of Western Europe and Japan at the end of World War II was relatively simple. In these areas were sophisticated, well-educated people, and an experienced reservoir of mature political leaders, civil servants, skilled workers, technicians, and business managers. What Europe and Japan needed was simply an injection of outside financial and food assistance until they could rebuild their war-damaged economies.

No such superstructure of education, civil service, and skills exists in most of the countries of Asia, Africa, and Latin America. Here, the task of development will be infinitely harder and the foreign assistance effort vastly more frustrating.

Expanding populations present another serious obstacle to economic development and more adequate diets. Modern sanitary techniques and the curbing of such killers as malaria have sharply curtailed the death rate, thus promoting rapid population increases.

Impoverished people engaged in primitive agriculture have retained the attitude that large families are an economic asset. Many children work at family labor from the age of eight or ten on. Also, children are the only form of old-age security that the parents have.

Four days after his inauguration, the late President John F. Kennedy created the White House Food for Peace Office and appointed Senator George S. McGovern of South Dakota its first Director.

Not far from the gleaming modern center of Hong Kong are acres of shanty towns such as this. Here hundreds of thousands of refugees from mainland China live in conditions of poverty which defy the imagination.

Senator McGovern and Arthur Schlesinger, Jr. were sent on a fact-finding mission to Latin America during the first weeks of the Kennedy administration. Here they inspect a slum village near Rio de Janeiro.

This very natural attitude in the agricultural areas is complicated by the longer life spans resulting from the successful attacks on epidemic diseases.

With populations growing as fast as national income, per capita income is static. The increase in people offsets increasing food production and aid offered by friendly countries. Consider the case of Latin America. This region now has a population of two hundred million, but at present growth rates another four hundred million will have been added by the year 2000. During the 1930's, Latin America was the largest grain-exporting region of the world. Today, it must import grain to survive.

This larger problem—the race between people and food—led Dr. Thomas Malthus to predict long ago that starvation was man's lot. Modern science has refuted Malthus to date, but if his prophecy is not to become a reality, Asia, Africa, and Latin America will have to undergo the kind of explosion in agriculture that is now taking place in population growth.

Still another obstacle to progress is the dependence of a number of countries on one or two commodities that fluctuate on the world market. These nations are dependent for capital and machinery for industrialization on selling primary products such as minerals, tropical fruits, coffee, tea, rubber, or hemp. The price of these materials has been decreasing in recent years while industrial prices have been rising. The loss to the poor nations between 1955 and 1961 because of these unfavorable terms of trade is estimated at $22 billion—

almost as much as the total aid extended to the under-developed world. World commodity market fluctuations have been undoing rather than supporting the efforts of our government and others to attack the problem of hunger and low income.

These are only a few of the major obstacles in the way of helping the people of the underdeveloped nations to eliminate the curse of hunger and the other social ills which follow in the wake of poverty. Taken together, they are large.

Recognizing the population growth ahead of us, total world food production will have to be doubled by 1980, and tripled by the year 2000. This is a much larger task than the immediate problem of closing the nutritional gap for the present population level. Yet, it is not beyond the capacity of the people of the earth to accomplish that huge job. During this century a number of nations, including Japan, Mexico, and Israel, have moved from hunger and want toward adequate diets.

The difficulties of ending world hunger are great, but the consequences of failure are even greater.

The Roman philosopher-statesman Seneca observed that "A hungry people listens not to reason, nor cares for justice, nor is bent by prayers." President Kennedy repeated this phrase at the World Food Congress in 1963, adding, "World peace and progress cannot be maintained in a world half fed and half hungry."

It does not take foresight to recognize that out of the hunger of the Brazilian village where we met the young mother and her doomed children may come not only misery and despair but violence and revolt. Long before another three billion people are added to the world's hungry, social and economic disorders could occur in dimensions we cannot fully comprehend.

Under such circumstances, the peace of the world would be far less certain. Gone would be the opportunity to help the hungry of the less-developed nations move toward a more abundant life through cooperative, peaceful effort rather than violence.

The mere absence of warfare in a world where half the people are hungry is not real peace. The seeming peace between World Wars I and II is now seen as an interlude in a half century of conflict that is still unsettled. A positive concept of peace includes a concerted attack on the chronic enemies of all men, of which hunger is the most basic. When man is as willing to sacrifice half as much in the war against hunger as he has in warring against his fellow humans, he will be able to replace hunger and misery with the things that make for peace.

CHAPTER II

Tools for the Attack

"There is no form of overseas assistance which this country is better able to provide than the supplying of American farm products and agricultural science."
—Dwight D. Eisenhower, July 24, 1960

THE people of the United States have not been indifferent to human hunger. Since the early years of the Republic, Americans, acting through both government and voluntary channels, have offered generous food assistance to other nations in times of crisis.

The first Federal appropriation for overseas disaster relief occurred on May 8, 1812, when Congress provided $50,000 for the purchase of food for victims of an earthquake in Venezuela.

During the Russian famine of 1891, privately donated food supplies from America prompted the mayor of St. Petersburg to exclaim, "When can true friendship be tested if not in the hour of misfortune!"

When in 1893-1894 the Turkish government severely suppressed civil disturbances in what came to be known as "the Armenian Massacres," the U.S. Armenian Relief

12

Committee contributed over $100,000 in food, clothing, and medicine to relieve the suffering.

American public opinion was strongly aroused a few years later when the Spanish herded large numbers of Cubans into concentration camps. Following a public appeal by President McKinley for donations of food, clothing, and funds, a Central Cuban Relief Committee was organized and the American Red Cross volunteered to administer the distribution of supplies.

The 1902 eruption of Mount Pelée on Martinique prompted the United States Congress to appropriate $200,000 for relief of the destitute people of the French West Indies. Congress also authorized the use of our Navy vessels to procure and distribute food, medicine, and clothing.

President Theodore Roosevelt did not wait for Congress to act before sending relief to the victims of the Sicilian earthquake of December 28, 1908. "Confident of your approval," he told Congress, "I have ordered the government supply ships *Celtic* and *Culgoa* to the scene of the disaster, where, upon receiving the authority which I now ask of you, they will be able to dispense food, clothing, and other supplies with which they are laden to the value of $300,000."

American food was shipped to India and China for famine relief on numerous occasions from 1890 to 1915. These famine relief requests became so frequent that, as early as the turn of the century, American relief agencies and government officials considered the possibility of famine prevention by technical assistance with foreign financing.

During and after World War I we sent vast supplies of food to a hungry Europe. That first major food relief effort got underway in 1914, when Belgium and northern France were invaded. This industrialized area, dependent upon food from abroad, was not only cut off from the usual sources of supply, but also suffered confiscation of its food reserves and crops by occupying forces. Ten million people faced starvation. Their lives were saved when American food was distributed through the Commission for Relief in Belgium. This magnificent enterprise, launched by President Woodrow Wilson, was directed by Herbert Hoover, the engineer who later became President.

In 1917, after the United States entered the war, food relief was expanded to include the United Kingdom and Italy. President Wilson established a Food Administration to encourage Americans to conserve food, to direct its distribution, and to stimulate greater production by our farmers.

The food relief task under Hoover did not end with the 1918 Armistice, for some two hundred million people in Europe were on the verge of starvation. To meet this crisis, food distribution organizations were created across Europe under the supervision of American military officers. The 1919 harvest in Europe helped ease the situation, and efforts were then directed toward relieving the hunger of some ten million undernourished children, many of them orphans, in central and eastern

Europe. Before the children's program was completed, a severe famine struck Russia in 1921. Throughout 1922 and 1923 American food and medical supplies poured in to save millions of Russian lives.

The magnificent food relief program of World War I covered almost a decade—November 1914 to July 1923. It is entirely understandable that Mr. Hoover should regard it as the outstanding achievement of his long life. Nearly thirty-four million tons of U.S. food and other relief supplies valued at $5.2 billion were delivered to twenty-three countries. In addition to U.S. Government funds, voluntary agencies spent millions of relief dollars contributed by private citizens, churches, and benevolent organizations.

With the coming of World War II, American food again played a decisive role. Following enactment of the Lend Lease Act in March 1941, our government procured vast quantities of food for the British. After our entry into the war at the end of 1941, our food shipments increased tremendously to fill the growing needs of the allied forces, including the Soviet Union. By the end of the war in 1945, we were procuring food for the war effort at the rate of $7 million a day. Our largest food relief activity of this period was conducted by the U.S. Army in occupied areas of Europe and Asia.

In both major conflicts of this century, American food was a crucial factor in allied victory. Likewise, in the wake of those devastating conflicts, the bounty of our farms and the humanitarianism of our citizenry averted widespread suffering and starvation. Each time

American farmers responded to appeals from their government for increased production in spite of wartime shortages of labor and materials. "Food will win the war and write the peace," exclaimed U.S. Secretary of Agriculture Claude Wickard.

It should be noted in passing that the plowing up of rangeland for wheat planting in World War I and the enormous increase in productivity of World War II have contributed to the farmer's dismay over mounting surpluses and falling prices in the 1920's and again in the 1950's and '60's. But the American farmer at least has the consolation of knowing that he was as important as any army in tipping the scales toward allied victory in 1918 and 1945.

After World War II, the voluntary agencies of the United States, particularly the church-connected groups, joined with the United Nations Relief and Rehabilitation Administration to distribute American food to the war-torn nations. Drought in 1946 and 1947 in many countries placed extraordinary demands on our farmers.

While American food was a matter of life or death for millions of people, it was in itself not enough to rebuild Europe's war-battered economy. In 1948, by a bipartisan vote, Congress approved President Truman's proposal to help rehabilitate Europe. Named "The Marshall Plan" after Secretary of State George Marshall, who first publicly announced the proposal in an address at Harvard University, it sent $13 billion in American resources into Western Europe in four years' time. A large part of this was food and fiber from our farms.

With these supplies and capital, Western Europe was able to rebuild its factories and farms and resume its food production. People took hope and resisted appeals for revolution and dictatorship.

One significant reason for the success of the Marshall Plan was that Europe, unlike the underdeveloped world, had the managerial skills, the trained labor, and the experienced public officials to convert aid into capital, and to rebuild a shattered economy into an operating system.

The Korean conflict, 1950-1953, necessitated a continued high level of farm production in the United States. But by 1954, with the war in Korea ended and the need for food assistance in Europe subsiding, farm surpluses began to accumulate in the United States. Farmers who had invested heavily in expanded, mechanized operations were unable to shut off production to protect their prices in the pattern of industrial corporations. To protect farm prices, the government agreed to take a portion of the surpluses off the market and place them in storage.

Faced with the problem of mounting food surpluses at home and chronic food shortages in many parts of the world, Congress enacted legislation in 1954 designed to utilize our food surpluses in the less-developed countries. This was the very important Agricultural Trade Development and Assistance Act of 1954, Public Law 480. Known the world around as "PL 480," it was an ingenious combination of self-interest and idealism. On the one hand, it was designed to assist American agriculture and the American taxpayer by providing an outlet for our farm surpluses and costly storages. On the other hand, it was a humanitarian effort to feed the hungry and promote the economic development of the poor nations. This was the double thrust that has made Public Law 480—the legislative base of Food for Peace —one of the most popular and successful programs ever authorized by Congress.

PL 480 provided three main channels for moving our surplus food to needy countries. The law clearly provided that American domestic needs be met first before food is made available for overseas use.

Title I of the law allows our government officials to make an arrangement with the government of a less-developed nation similar to the process used under the Marshall Plan. The receiving government lacking dollars or gold pays in its own currency at the export market value of the product. The local government then sells the food to its wholesalers and retailers. The United States has granted or loaned back about 80 percent of the currency for economic development, mutual defense, and other purposes. For example, in India, some of the rupees from the sale of wheat have been used in a successful malaria eradication campaign.

Some of the money reserved by the American government from every Title I sale has been used to develop commercial markets for American food and fiber, as loans to our businessmen overseas, and for such programs as Fulbright fellowships, the translation of scientific journals, the U.S. Information Service, and the maintenance of our embassies.

Of the approximately $9 billion in foreign currency which we have derived through Food for Peace sales, $7 billion has been loaned or granted to the receiving countries for approved purposes. The remaining $2 billion has been reserved for American uses.

More than one-third of the entire American economic aid program now consists of Food for Peace—70 percent of this under Title I foreign currency sales. In this way, our farm surpluses and the currencies which they generate are being converted into classrooms, clinics, dams, and roads in the needy nations.

The second tool we use in the attack on world hunger is Title II of the Food for Peace law, which authorizes our government to make outright grants of food in emergencies or disasters, such as drought or floods. Millions of people in every part of the world have been lifted from the depths of despair by timely grants of disaster food relief. Food grants may also be used for economic development projects, the payment of wages, or school lunch programs. About $1¼ billion of commodities in export market value have been shipped under this grant section.

Typical of the aid we are giving under this phase of Food for Peace is our effort in Algeria, where four million people were uprooted by the long war of independence. American wheat, milk, and oil are now being used to pay the wages of Algerians reconstructing their country.

There is a growing trend away from straight food donations to the use of food as wage payments. In twenty-two countries, 700,000 men are now working for food wages. In addition, food is being used to "grub-stake" farm families who are opening up new farmlands.

One exciting development which holds great promise for the future is the use of food to finance youth work camps to combat juvenile delinquency and teen-age idleness.

The third section of Public Law 480 authorizes the distribution abroad of surplus food by private voluntary agencies such as CARE, and a score of church-connected agencies, including Church World Service, Catholic Relief Services, Lutheran World Relief, the Jewish Joint Distribution Committee, the Quakers, and the Mennonites. They provide supplemental feeding for approximately seventy million people in 112 countries and territories. Contributions from their own members and supporters cover administrative costs.

Since 1954, flour, cornmeal, powdered milk, rice, cheese, and edible oils worth $2½ billion at export market value have been distributed by our private agencies under Title III. Their magnificent achievements stretch across the world from Hong Kong to Calcutta, from Algiers to Lima.

Title III also permits the barter of food for foreign strategic materials.

After five years of operation, in 1959 a fourth tool was added to PL 480—the extension of long-term credit at low interest rates on dollar sales of surplus food and fiber. It was believed that some countries were moving into a position where they would be able to pay dollars for food if favorable credit terms could be extended. Although this authority was not used until 1961, agreements for the sale of food valued at $145 million have been completed.

These are the four tools of the Food for Peace program.

Since 1954, with the enactment of Public Law 480, we have sent a growing volume of food to the developing nations. Under the law, 120 million tons of food valued at $13 billion—enough to fill three large ships each day for ten years—have flowed overseas from American farms. This represents 27 percent of all U.S. agricultural exports. Two-thirds of our wheat exports have been through Food for Peace channels.

Leaving aside barter and dollar sales, which are almost pure commercial arrangements, in the seven years between 1954 and 1961 the average rate of food exports under PL 480 was $891 million per year. In the three years since mid-1961, the average rate was $1.4 billion. This increase of 60 percent over the previous seven-year average is a considerable advance in the attack on hunger since the 1961 Executive Order by President Kennedy calling for a maximum effort. President Eisenhower had earlier given a significant thrust to Food for Peace in a 1959 message to Congress and through the appointment of an able White House coordinator, Dr. Don Paarlberg.

A requirement by Congress that a specified percentage of foreign aid appropriations be used to purchase farm commodities added $2 billion to Food for Peace. With the $5 billion in food during the Marshall Plan, the total of all U.S. overseas food assistance since 1948 is over $20 billion.

There is no parallel in human history for this massive movement of food. It has largely put an end to death-dealing famine in our age. It has given an enormous lift to war-torn Europe and Japan and has contributed beyond measure to the strength, hope, and health of the great masses of humanity struggling to get on their feet in Asia, Latin America, and Africa.

Today, one hundred million people throughout the world benefit directly from the American Food for Peace effort. Several times that number benefit indirectly. This is an achievement that may rank as high in history as any of our recent scientific accomplishments. While it is a humanitarian venture of the highest order, it has also been of great benefit to the American people.

The food resources we have been moving abroad resulted from our efforts to help the American farmer. Surpluses acquired by the government under the price support program in the 1950's were soon costing the nation over a million dollars a day in storage charges alone. Those surpluses and storage charges would have been twice as large were it not for Food for Peace outlets.

Furthermore, with these much heavier surplus stocks overhanging our domestic market, American farm income would have been seriously depressed. One out of every three acres of American wheat goes into Food for Peace. What would we do with these acres and the farm families who cultivate them in the absence of overseas food programs?

Food for Peace has resulted in substantial income to our economy as a whole, including the suppliers of farm machinery, seeds, fertilizer, and insecticides. It has meant an additional $1.4 billion to the American shipping industry.

Half of the total bookkeeping cost of $18 billion in Food for Peace since 1954 can properly be allocated to the fight against hunger, and the other half to our agricultural economy. This represents $1 billion a year to fight hunger over the nine-year period, or $5.65 per person. In view of the magnitude of the problem and the challenge which world hunger presents to peace, growth, and freedom, this cannot be considered unreasonable.

There are other important compensations to the United States from Food for Peace. Currencies generated by the sales now save us nearly $300 million annually in foreign exchange, which helps our balance of payments situation to that extent. Furthermore, a sizable portion of the local currency which we have loaned to host governments will be repaid.

Food for Peace has also served important foreign policy objectives of the United States. For example, in 1957 President Eisenhower authorized American food aid to Poland and Yugoslavia. Since then, Poland has received $671 million in food, and Yugoslavia $906 million. An important result has been to encourage these two quasi-Communist states to maintain a remarkable degree of independence from the Soviet Union.

An interesting by-product of our food shipments to Poland and Yugoslavia is that both countries have discarded the Communist technique of trying to raise farm products through government collectives. They have moved back toward private family farms which are apparently far more successful than the Russian government collectives. Our surpluses may be helping those two nations to show not only their people but also the Russians that independent family farming is superior to collectivism.

Food for Peace has contributed further to our national interest by developing new commercial marketing opportunities. A substantial part of the proceeds of foreign currency sales has been used to advertise and promote American farm products. Many of our private commercial organizations have cooperated with the government in sponsoring trade fairs and other market promotional activities abroad.

Before we enter into a Food for Peace arrangement, we consult with other exporting nations to make certain that their markets are not disturbed. Our own exporters are also protected. The normal commercial purchases of the receiving country must be continued as a condition of our food assistance.

Through Food for Peace, we have introduced our

commodities to countries that will one day be commercial purchasers. Japan, Italy, Spain, and others have already moved from Food for Peace recipients to strong dollar customers. Japanese school children who learned to like American milk and bread in U.S.-sponsored school lunch programs have since helped to make Japan our best dollar purchaser for farm products.

The great food markets of the future are the very areas where vast numbers of people are learning through Food for Peace to eat American produce.

The people we assist today will become our customers tomorrow. Our best markets are in those nations with the most developed agricultural and industrial economies. Canada, with a population one-twentieth the size of India's, purchases far more American produce than does the vast populace of India. An enormous market for American produce of all kinds will come into being if India can achieve even half the productivity of Canada.

We have looked briefly at the challenge of world hunger, some of the obstacles in meeting that challenge, and the Food for Peace tools we have fashioned.

Now the time has come to travel around the world to see how we are feeding hungry people and using food as an instrument of development.

CHAPTER III

Serving the Food for Peace Table

"We all share responsibility for the fact that populations are undernourished. Therefore, it is necessary to arouse a sense of responsibility in individuals, especially among those more blessed with this world's goods."
—Encyclical of Pope John XXIII, *Mater et Magistra*

"GIVE us this day our daily bread" is for millions of Americans a prayer of thanksgiving for bountiful food. But for the *campesino* in northeast Brazil, the child in the streets of Calcutta, the weary mother in an African village, it is a cry born of hunger. That cry has been heard by the American people, and they have responded more generously than any nation in history.

Thanks to the donation channels of Food for Peace, a hundred million people in 114 countries and territories are now guests at our table. Among them are forty million school children receiving daily school lunches in eighty countries. Among them, too, are millions of preschool children, nursing mothers, refugees, needy families, and victims of disaster.

To view any one of the eager guests at this great table and see light coming back to eyes dulled by undernourishment is a deeply moving experience.

Ministering to these guests around the world are the American private voluntary agencies. Largely through these groups, our powdered milk, cornmeal, flour, edible oils, and other food gifts are distributed to the needy overseas.

Most Americans and millions of people in the neglected parts of the world are familiar with the humanitarian mission of CARE, the Red Cross, Church World Service, Catholic Relief Services, Lutheran World Relief, the Jewish Joint Distribution Committee, and such United Nations affiliates as UNICEF and UNRWA. Through the world service arm of their churches and benevolent organizations, tens of millions of Americans stretch their arms around the globe in a mission to the hungry. But few are aware of the volume of food and services that these agencies transmit.

Our humanitarian and religious groups cooperating in Food for Peace are now distributing three billion pounds of food yearly. Reaching approximately seventy million persons in 112 countries and territories, they have distributed over fifteen billion pounds of food since 1950, when they received the first commodities under the Agricultural Act of 1949. Included in the recipients are fifty-five million children—some thirty-two million in school lunch programs.

The private groups have taken a steadily growing role in food distribution since the enactment of Public Law 480 in 1954. In recent years, they have increasingly emphasized the coordination of food aid with community development self-help projects. Food has been used along with technical guidance to encourage the building of projects such as wells, sanitation facilities, clinics, schools, and roads.

The great strength of the voluntary groups as compared to direct government programs is their ability to humanize foreign assistance. The warmth of a hand or the joy of a smile can transform a coldly impersonal foreign aid program into a heart-warming relationship between human beings.

Voluntarism is a deep-seated pattern of American life that expresses our democratic heritage and our strong missionary tradition. During the past quarter of a century, since the 1939 Nazi invasion of Poland, Americans have voluntarily contributed through their humanitarian and religious agencies $3½ billion for overseas aid. World War II, with the cruel invasions by the Axis powers, brought a flood of appeals to the American people for help. War relief committees sprang up by the score across the nation.

Since the United States had a neutral status to preserve in the early years of the war, all voluntary groups engaged in the relief of belligerent countries were required to register with the Department of State. President Franklin D. Roosevelt named a committee on March 13, 1941, to evaluate the problems of war relief activities, and from this study came the President's War Relief Control Board, established by Executive Order on July 25, 1942, to guide the agencies in their activities. On May 14, 1946, the board was replaced by the present Advisory Committee on Voluntary Foreign Aid established by President Truman.

Fifty-three groups, sectarian and nonsectarian, maintain overseas aid programs—with half of them involved in food distribution. Thirty-nine of these associations of American citizens have attempted an informal sharing of their common problem through the formation of the American Council of Voluntary Agencies for Foreign Service. With headquarters in New York City, the council maintains a small executive staff guided by officers elected annually from the member agencies.

Each voluntary agency participating in the Food for Peace program is first approved by the government-designated committee of private citizens—the Advisory Committee on Voluntary Foreign Aid. Operations are carefully reviewed by government officials in the Agency for International Development and the Department of Agriculture. In addition, each group must maintain at least one American supervisor in the receiving country. At present, eight hundred Americans are assigned to overseas responsibilities assisted by four thousand native employees—paid by the agencies. Countless thousands of additional unpaid native volunteers assist in the food distribution.

As an example of how the agencies accomplish their task, Church World Service, organized in 1946, has brought together a number of the Protestant church-related overseas rehabilitation groups. It has been able to enlist the assistance of more than ten thousand church members overseas who have volunteered their services. Church World Service has a very small paid staff abroad and in the United States giving full-time direction to its efforts. Many of the paid employees overseas, especially in technical assistance efforts, are supplied by other governments, religious groups abroad, or the World Council of Churches.

I have been asked frequently if the people we are feeding are aware that the United States is assisting them. The answer is "yes" in the case of nearly all our voluntary agency operations, including the school lunch programs.

Every package of food donated abroad is clearly labeled in English and in the language of the receiving country: "Donated by the people of the United States." Posters are also displayed at the distribution points to indicate the American source of the food.

Doubtless, our private agencies, including the church-related groups, receive some organizational benefit for their efforts as well as the credit they reflect on our country. But regulations require that the food not be used in any way to promote a particular religious doctrine. It must be made available on the basis of need without reference to creed, color, or race.

The relationship of the voluntary agencies to the government has been a most effective Food for Peace partnership. The government provides the commodities in suitable packages and pays the ocean freight to the foreign port. The agency then takes over to provide the distribution of the food abroad. The receiving country's government pays the cost of inland freight plus port and storage charges. This arrangement has been a satisfactory one generally, although not entirely free of controversy.

There is some anxiety on the part of a very few of the church-related agency spokesmen as to the proper proportion of government investment in any given program. They have suggested that the private, voluntary character of a church-related effort might be lost if the government investment were to exceed substantially more than half the cost of the program. On the other hand, the agencies as a whole would like to see the government broaden the programs by assisting in the purchase of utensils, tools, and other facilities needed in the distribution of food.

In spite of these differences, the private agencies have strongly reinforced each other and the government aid programs as well.

The brightest chapter in the voluntary program and, indeed, in the entire Food for Peace effort, is the international school lunch program.

Although some of the forty million children now receiving school lunches daily are fed in direct government programs, well over three-fourths of them receive their lunches through one of the voluntary associations.

Usually the lunch is meager fare compared to our domestic program. In many cases, it consists of a roll and a glass of reconstituted nonfat dry milk. Yet, for most of the recipients this is the only nourishing meal of their day. Sometimes it is supplemented by vegetables, fruit, or meat added by the local parents or school officials. The results have been nothing less than spectacular both in terms of better health and sharply improved academic growth.

The relationship of a good school lunch program to the physical health of children is well known. In our own country school lunches have contributed enormously to the strength and energy of our students. The dean of one of our Southern universities once told me that in his opinion the school lunch program had done more to strengthen the health and well-being of the South than any other federally assisted program in the last quarter of a century.

One can only imagine how much sharper is the impact of a school feeding program in underdeveloped countries where the meals at home are more meager than in the poorest homes in the United States.

Even in postwar Japan, where the economy and the diet were better than in most countries, a U.S.-assisted school lunch program added inches and pounds to the average size of Japanese youth. Japanese school officials have been forced to install larger desks because the children of this generation are larger than their mothers and fathers.

What is not so well known is the striking effect of school lunches in attendance and academic performance. Yet, in country after country students have shown a remarkable academic improvement and attendance has improved by as much as 50 percent. The reasons are not difficult to understand. Millions of children simply do not have the energy to remain in school.

Those who do continue are often so undernourished and listless that learning is next to impossible. School lunches dramatically change these conditions.

Years ago, the late Prime Minister Nehru observed: "You cannot talk of God to a starving person; you must give him food." It is equally true that you cannot teach reading and writing and history and government to hungry children.

It is not easy, however, to run a well-managed school lunch program in an underdeveloped country. It involves advance arrangements with the local governments that pay transportation and sometimes preparation and distribution costs. The products have to be adequately stored. A bakery has to be secured to bake the rolls. Care has to be taken to keep the milk clean. Utensils and facilities for washing them have to be provided. Any theft of the products and their sale on the open market involves protests from local producers and retailers of food. Worry lest the supply of food be interrupted is always present. When parents contribute foods or when cornmeal or bulgur wheat is added, cooking facilities must be supplied and people to do the cooking and prepare the food as well.

Any American who has participated in one of our domestic school lunch programs can appreciate how difficult it would be to operate such a program in an area where clean water and the simplest of utensils are not available. Voluntary agency representatives have to be diligent, dedicated public servants.

Shortly before I visited the U.S.-assisted school lunch

program in the State of Madras, India—an excellent
program supervised by CARE—several children died
after consuming U.S. reconstituted milk powder. At
first, fear swept across the country that the American
milk was toxic. Investigation revealed, however, that a
kettle of milk curd left uncovered overnight was con-
taminated by a foreign substance.

One of the most impressive of the voluntary agency
feeding programs is the far-reaching effort in Egypt.

The great majority of Egypt's twenty-six million
people gain a living from a narrow strip of land along
the Nile, the delta, and the canal zone. The peasants,
or fellahin, cultivate the land much as they did in the
days of the Pharaohs. They are extremely poor. Egyp-
tians receive 650 pounds of food yearly per capita, compared to our 1,450 pounds. And it is not adequate food.
There is chronic malnutrition throughout the land.

At the Egyptian government's invitation, a Food for
Peace school feeding program was initiated by CARE
in 1954. School attendance skyrocketed and academic
performance improved rapidly as hungry, listless children gained new energy and spirit from American milk
and rolls.

CARE's program in Egypt now reaches three million
children. In addition, Church World Service and Catholic Relief Services are feeding half a million others.
Some of these are in the Gaza Strip and include refugees, nursing mothers, and needy families.

During a visit to Cairo in early 1962, I was deeply
moved by the striking impact of our Food for Peace

efforts. Nearly 90 percent of U.S. aid to Egypt is food and fiber—a combination of soft-currency sales plus grants through the voluntary agencies. To visit almost any classroom in Cairo at lunch time and see a little child raise to his lips a tin cup of American milk while clutching a roll is a heart-warming experience. I shall never forget the sea of smiling young faces that I saw in the classrooms of Cairo.

Exciting by-products have come from the large school feeding program in the Philippines, now reaching four and a half million children. With the launching of the school program, the American Food for Peace sponsors provided mobile medical units to treat beriberi and intestinal parasites prevalent among the children.

These mobile vans have reached the most remote communities. Some 535 rural schools furnished with medical kits now serve as first aid stations for all the people in the surrounding rural areas, where there are no doctors. One useful service thus made another one possible.

One of the most remarkable schools in the world is the Oriental Boat Mission of Hong Kong harbor. It serves as a school for 240 small sons and daughters of Chinese fisherfolk who live on junks and sampans, joined together in a vast floating city. The monthly tuition is $2 for a morning session and $1 for an afternoon session. These small fees pay the salaries of the Chinese teachers. The Mennonite Church agency in Hong Kong prepares the meals for the children from

Food for Peace stocks plus luncheon meat donated by the government of Canada and American Mennonites.

As our mission watched, a slim Chinese girl drew alongside the school boat in a skiff carrying a pair of steaming aluminum kettles. The food inside was a fluffy white bed of rice dotted with darker-colored U.S. bulgar wheat. A thick savory soup of onions, tomatoes, beans, and meat carried a mouth-watering odor into all the corners of the two classrooms of the boat. For the children it was the happiest time of the day—their midday meal. Members of our touring mission who witnessed that scene will always know that American aid can warm the heart, light the eyes, and ease the burden of otherwise neglected children.

Fortunately for the children of the world our school lunch programs are growing at a fairly rapid pace. In sheer numbers of school children receiving U.S. food, India heads the list with nine million, followed by the Philippines and Brazil with four and a half million each, Egypt with three and a half million, and Mexico and Korea with two million each.

By regions, South Asia is first with 11.3 million school lunch recipients, Latin America has ten million, the Far East 7.1 million, the Near East 4.9 million, Europe four million, and Africa 1.7 million.

If we were to reach every needy school child with a daily Food for Peace lunch, we would doubtless have to increase our program tenfold. The principal barrier to that undertaking is the inability or unwillingness of the receiving countries to underwrite their portion of such a vast effort. It is an exciting prospect, however, and should be considered as a possible long-term goal.

The governments, lacking funds for economic growth, are being pressed by the parents to move our food supplies to their children. They are not always able to move as rapidly as they would like. But in 1963 the governments of Latin America alone invested $13 million in the school lunch programs supported by Food for Peace. Similarly the voluntary agencies must obtain funds before they can pay their staffs and perform their supervisory function.

The American people ought to draw considerable satisfaction from the knowledge that our food assistance is enabling millions of children to develop stronger bodies and minds before they take on the responsibilities of adulthood. We are making an investment in human beings who will determine the future of their societies. Human capital is ultimately the most important capital, and educated and healthy children are the basic requirements for any effective society.

In inaugurating one of our finest Food for Peace school lunch programs, American Ambassador John Kenneth Galbraith told the people of Madras, India: "It is good that we have light in our lamps. It is even better that we have light in our children's eyes. I hope that those who look at the power plants of the Five-Year Plans will also spare a glance at the children who are better fed and better read as a result of the progressive vision of the people of Madras."

After observing U.S. foreign aid operations the world

around, I have concluded that no other single effort returns such high dividends as our Food for Peace school lunch program, now reaching forty million children. I hope we can at least triple that program in the years ahead. What greater investment can we make than to convert our agricultural abundance into healthier, happier, and more useful boys and girls?

There are other satisfactions for those who are helping in the voluntary agency feeding programs.

In Senegal, the healing of lepers is aided by our food donations. Some eight thousand persons suffering from this dread disease are believed hidden among the population. Under the supervision of American voluntary agency personnel, trucks driven by men cured of the disease carry food to known lepers. U.S. food is thus encouraging the afflicted to come forward for help. In this way, a disease which can be cured if properly treated is being sharply reduced.

A similar by-product has been achieved in the little African Republic of Chad. Social workers and doctors distributing milk were able to use the occasion to dispense drugs for malaria and other diseases.

The way in which the knowledge of the curative powers of milk spreads is exciting evidence of the possibility of progress in the underdeveloped areas. In Ghana, as in other parts of Africa, *kwashiorkor*—a disease stemming from protein deficiency—saps the capacity of its victims to face even simple human responsibilities. Preying primarily on children between the weaning period and the age of six, it is recognized by the gaunt limbs and distended belly so prevalent in Africa. Yet, in three or four weeks the child receiving American-donated milk shows miraculous improvement.

In the free city of Hong Kong on the edge of Communist China, a million refugees from the mainland have jammed into an already overcrowded city. Hundreds of thousands live on the sidewalks, the rooftops, in squatter huts, or on floating sampans. Sixty thousand tuberculosis sufferers cough away their lives. Thousands of orphaned street urchins scrounge the streets and alleys for food. Half a million men, women, and children—largely refugees from Red China—survive on U.S. food rations now being distributed by half a dozen American agencies.

Operations in Hong Kong were at first hampered by the Chinese dietary traditions that led them to frown on our milk powder, cornmeal, and flour. This problem has been largely solved by the development of a simple noodle-making machine to convert our food into a form more suited to the oriental taste. The noodle machine, developed by Monsignor Romaniello of Catholic Relief Services, calls for a mixture of 75 percent wheat flour, 20 percent cornmeal, and 5 percent nonfat dry milk powder.

Catholic Relief Services, Lutheran World Relief, CARE, and other agencies are operating life-saving programs in this crucial city.

All of these varied efforts by our voluntary benevolent and religious groups participating in Food for Peace represent human beings working with their fellow hu-

mans in an area of common concern. While the administration of the program is seldom free from problems
and even some failure, there is little or no corruption.
The agencies are becoming more effective each year in
the handling, preparation, and distribution of foods.
Black-market operations still exist, but only on a very
small scale.

When we think of forty million school children and
another sixty million human beings who are being given
food from the abundance of our farms we can be proud
that we have found this way to help malnourished people to a better life with new hope for the future. At
times we may not approve of their governments, but
poor people, and particularly the children, receiving
our food should not be punished for what we conceive
to be the sins of their governments. They have very
little to say about those governments at present. Children as well as underprivileged adults will suffer enough
from poor local government without our punishing them
for political reasons.

The same consideration ought to govern our actions
in responding to disasters or emergencies, and indeed,
the American people have so responded.

Famine, drought, flood, volcanoes, and earthquakes
have all brought our Food for Peace cooperating agencies into the field. Emergency grants of food are authorized under Title II of PL 480. This power to respond
quickly to emergencies is a vital one. The speedy
arrival of America's Globemaster planes loaded with
food in the wake of a disastrous earthquake in Chile in

These homeless children sleeping on the sidewalks of Bombay have millions of counterparts in large tropical and sub-tropical cities throughout the world.

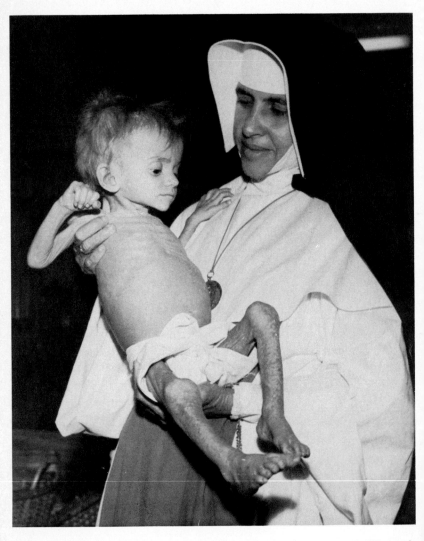

Sister Dulce Lopez Pontes, founder of the Albergue Santo Antonio Hospital in Bahia State, Brazil, cradles an emaciated child in her arms. Sister Dulce typifies the dedicated men and women throughout the world who wage war on famine through private and church-related volunteer agencies.

1960 was reported by observers on the scene to have done more for U.S.-Chilean relations than any other single American action in recent years. This is typical of hundreds of such emergency Food for Peace grants.

Early in 1961, serious famine conditions developed among 300,000 Baluba tribesmen in the Kasai Province of the Congo. Thousands of men, women, and children were reduced to living skeletons. Twelve hundred undernourished or starving patients jammed a 150-bed hospital in the city of Bakwanga. Nursing mothers had no milk for their babies. Scores of hungry refugees with lowered resistance fell victims to contagious diseases.

The authorities resorted to mass burials in South Kasai, where as many as two hundred persons died daily from starvation and attendant diseases. Some Baluba parents saw several of their children buried at one time in hastily dug common graves. These appalling conditions worsened as more refugees arrived. Local resources were depleted and supplies of the Red Cross and the missionaries were inadequate to meet the disaster situation. Airplanes chartered by the United Nations staff could not bring enough food from neighboring countries to meet the need.

Then on January 25, President Kennedy announced that the United States would meet emergency needs for food in that strife-torn area. United States Air Force planes began to arrive with food and medicine. These gave the United Nations medical staff and nutritionists the supplies they needed. In addition, Globemasters ferried in quantities of seed, which the Balubans quickly planted. By February, enough food was stored in Bakwanga to meet immediate needs. Further supplies were on their way by rail, river, and road from Matadi, a Congo River port with access to the Atlantic.

Meanwhile, a rapidly organized and efficient distribution program was set up by U.N. personnel. Necessary foods were issued weekly to every family in the 3,500-square-mile famine area. Hot meals were served at feeding stations to children, to expectant mothers, and to the aged. U.S. powdered milk was reconstituted and distributed daily to Baluba children, who by midyear were healthy and well fed. Almost vanished from the region was the evidence of *kwashiorkor*, the ubiquitous protein deficiency disease which had brought death to many children during the famine. The patient loads at the hospitals and clinics dropped to normal, crops began flourishing, and the remaining American foodstuffs were turned over to the United Nations staff for sale to finance public works projects for some fifty thousand needy persons. The Food for Peace program after this emergency was switched from feeding the hungry to giving work, and thereby creating capital.

The Congo in 1961 or the earthquake in Chile and other such disasters are clearly emergency situations requiring quick, decisive action. What we confront throughout much of the world is chronic need unaccompanied by any disaster of nature. But the line between misery caused by acts of nature and that caused by the inadequacies of society is thin. The results are alike.

Indeed, misery resulting from the actions or inactions of men seems to endure longer.

Fortunately, chronic malnutrition, especially among children, is beginning to challenge us as strongly as a flood, a drought, or an earthquake.

Evidence of the growing response of private citizens to the challenge of hunger is the work of the Food for Peace Council. This group of Americans, named by the President and representing farm, labor, business, religious, and professional people, serves as an advisory council to the Food for Peace Director. Under the chairmanship of Paul S. Willis, president of the Grocery Manufacturers Association, the council has assumed an increasingly important role. Its members, who serve without pay, have offered helpful insights and have served as a two-way channel of information between the government and the American public. The council has sponsored several regional and national public forums.

The first meeting of the Food for Peace Council in Washington on June 28, 1961, was highlighted by an impromptu appearance of President Kennedy. Shortly after the participants had assembled in the International Conference Room of the Department of State, Mr. Kennedy completed a press conference in the auditorium nearby. As he was leaving the auditorium a secretary in the Food for Peace office asked him if he would say a few words to the conference then in progress. Mr. Kennedy agreed, strode onto the stage and delivered a moving, impromptu statement which those present will never forget.

"I recognize," he said, "that you people in coming here today are not only fulfilling a responsibility, but that you are participating in a great adventure of the human race, which is to feed those who are not fed, to shelter those who are not sheltered, to use our great strength to help those who are not strong."

When then Vice President Johnson visited Pakistan in 1961, he met a congenial camel driver, Bashir, whom he later induced to come to the United States as his guest. During a brief visit to my office, Bashir told me that there is an old adage in Pakistan which goes something as follows: "If there are two brothers and the one has much food while the other has little, their work will go much better if the one with much shares with the one who has little."

Through the channels of many voluntary and government agencies, Food for Peace is advancing that view.

CHAPTER IV

Food: Instrument of Economic Development

*"The scientific and technological revolution in agriculture
has opened the door to the possibility of plenty under which
no man, woman, or child need be in want.... The challenge
we face is to open wider the gate to this era of abundance."*
—U.S. Secretary of Agriculture Orville Freeman

IN recent years, we have been using food more and
more as a tool of economic and social development—a
most hopeful trend in the evolution of Food for Peace.

Public Law 480, on which our Food for Peace program is based, was originally conceived in 1954, largely
as a means of disposing of the mounting agricultural
surpluses for foreign currencies when their sale abroad
for dollars proved impossible. Economic development
was listed in an ill-defined manner as one of many uses
of the foreign currencies which could not be converted
to dollars and repatriated.

But, over the years, the underdeveloped countries
have come to rely on the PL 480 program for supplies
of food and fiber to assist economic development. This
has been largely for the purpose of saving development

45

plans from ruinous inflation because of food shortages and not a positive program in which the agricultural surpluses would promote projects to provide mass employment and economic betterment for the depressed and needy of the underdeveloped countries.

The importance of food for economic development is now generally recognized. A shortage of food is one of the main barriers to satisfactory economic development in most underdeveloped countries. The reason is simple. The people live on a subsistence level. Most of their meager incomes are spent on food and clothing. Various studies indicate that two-thirds of consumer expenditures in underdeveloped countries is for this purpose. This is, of course, a universal law of economic development. An 1875 survey on consumer expenditures of American working families showed that 75 percent of their income was spent on food and clothing.

The importance of food as an essential resource for economic development can be seen in the consumption pattern in underdeveloped countries. Unfortunately, only a few of them have developed refined statistics. But these clearly reveal the importance of food in the underdeveloped economy.

The National Sample Surveys of India found that 61.3 percent of consumer expenditure in India was for food. In the rural areas, it was 64.1 percent and in the urban areas, 51.5 percent. Next in importance was clothing.

More to the point, however, are the two Enquiries on Agriculture Labour in India of 1951 and 1957. They consist of broad studies on the conditions of the most depressed group in the Indian society (comprising today about seventy million people) dependent on agricultural labor or marginal cultivation or both for their livelihood. This is the real problem group in each underdeveloped country—the manpower which is surplus to agriculture and not yet absorbed by industry. The consumption pattern of the agricultural laborers was found to be as follows:

	1951 Enquiry	1957 Enquiry
Food	85.3%	77.3%
Clothing and footwear	6.3%	6.1%
Fuel and lighting	1.1%	7.9%
Services and miscellaneous	7.3%	8.7%
	100.0%	100.0%

As underdeveloped countries undertake economic development, new jobs and greater incomes are created which increase the demand for food. This is further aggravated by inordinate population growth resulting primarily from the introduction of public health measures under the development plans which decrease the death rate. Meanwhile, domestic production of food lags for a variety of reasons and the result is a food shortage which sooner or later retards satisfactory economic development.

The underdeveloped country is unable to provide full-time jobs for all its people to enable them to earn a satisfactory wage for adequate subsistence. Yet, the country needs social and economic facilities such as housing, hospitals, schools, roads, and agricultural improvements for which this idle manpower could be utilized. But if such social development were undertaken, providing greater employment for the depressed people, the newly created incomes would be spent largely for food that could not be supplied by domestic agriculture. Food prices would soar, rendering the economic betterment illusory.

Lacking the necessary food resources required by such social development projects, most underdeveloped countries forgo them. The alternative is often spectacular industrialization, which fails to improve the economic conditions of the people. And in many instances, the successful industrialization even worsens the lot of many as it is frequently accompanied by inflation, primarily in the form of increased food prices caused by growing demand for inadequate food supplies by the new industrial wage earners.

Industrialization provides little employment, as it is capital intensive. Meanwhile, the underemployed in the rural areas find their food prices rising and their lot worsening. This is the source of much of the social and political unrest in Latin America, Africa, and Asia.

Food and fiber from outside can alleviate this situation during the early stages of economic development before domestic agricultural production increases to meet the growing demand. It can not only stem rising food prices but, if proffered on a large scale, enable the underdeveloped country to undertake labor-intensive projects such as rural roads, housing, dispensaries, and agricultural improvements which will generate more employment and economic betterment for the under-employed.

The dynamic use of food as a capital contribution to economic development is capturing the enthusiasm of our foreign aid officials and the receiving countries. Food for Peace agreements are now being carefully coordinated with the individual country development plans.

The food input stimulates development indirectly in various ways. It provides the physical energy that workers must have for more effective labor. It checks what would otherwise be a painful inflation of food prices set off by the stimulus of development projects and increased wages. It helps to conserve the foreign exchange of both the assisting and the receiving country while introducing larger quantities of food, more nutritious diets, and healthier workers.

These are the indirect economic benefits of food assistance. But food can also be used directly as capital in the financing of development projects. This is being accomplished by paying workers partly in food or by selling the food and using the proceeds for wages. Currencies generated from the Title I food sales have been widely used, largely to finance the building of roads, schools, dams, sanitation systems, medical facilities, and other vital programs approved by our aid mission and the host country. Much of the Indian development program depends on Food for Peace capital. Indeed, half of all American aid to India has been food.

The food-for-wages formula is not as flexible or as simple to administer as the use of local currency; but it provides another development tool which is especially helpful in many areas of the world.

Today in twenty-two countries, 700,000 workers—the bread-earners for families totaling four million people —are employed in capital-creating self-help projects for which they are paid partially with our food. Not only are hungry people fed, but they are building up the basic structure necessary for the economic growth of their nations. Wheat from Kansas and the Dakotas is being converted into schools in Bolivia, and milk from Wisconsin is building roads in Iran.

These self-help programs, which create precious social and economic capital, began on a pilot scale in Tunisia on the southern edge of the Mediterranean in 1958.

In central Tunisia, the traveler sees miles of desert landscape, acres of esparto grass and then—miraculously —cultivated plots appear with freshly planted fruit and olive trees.

The transformation of the Tunisian landscape from barren desert to productive orchards and farms has resulted from the work of such men as Ahmed Ben Taieb. Before the land reclamation program was undertaken in this region, he was unemployed—one of nearly 400,000, or one-third of Tunisia's "active" male population, out of work.

He now works six days a week, earns a daily wage equal to 67 cents. Formerly illiterate, Ahmed Ben Taieb spends an hour in an adult education class learning to read and write as part of his regular workday.

He collects his monetary wage, which is about 45 cents daily, and receives food coupons for the balance. Once a week he goes to the village of El Djem to pick up his food allotment—3½ pounds of semolina (a wheat cereal) for each day's work, an amount considered to be the normal consumption for a worker and his dependents.

Ahmed Ben Taieb is one of some 170,000 workers engaged in similar economic development projects throughout Tunisia who receive food from United States supplies as a portion of their wages. His story illustrates how Food for Peace has helped to reduce Tunisian unemployment and strengthen the country's economic independence.

Started as a pilot program at the suggestion of Tunisian President Bourguiba, the projects are referred to by the Tunisians as "La Lutte Contre le Sous-Développement—(The Battle Against Underdevelopment).

Land improvement, reforestation, and construction of hospitals, schools, clinics, low-cost housing, and roads are all in progress. This is the kind of "social capital" that an underdeveloped country needs before it can attract private capital investment. American wheat and soybean oil are financing a sizable part of it.

The average person employed is given about three pounds of wheat semolina and 50 cents in cash for each day's work. This is the food-for-work program, the transformation of food into capital, which has been taken as a model by other countries, including Morocco, Ethiopia, Iran, Algeria, Brazil, Korea, and Ecuador.

The government of Tunisia is using some of the currency generated by Title I Food for Peace sales to pay part of the wages and other project costs. It has been careful not to allow the program to become a permanent pattern and has insisted that people working on such projects get into the private monetary sectors of the economy as fast as job opportunities permit. The government is now planning to transfer more than 90,000 workers to cash jobs.

In neighboring Morocco, the food-for-wages project is called the "program of national promotion." At its beginning in June of 1961 tools and materials were lacking; so some of the food was sold to secure needed supplies. The Moroccan government pays a cash supplement to the wages and operates the program with some technical aid from the United States. Irrigation, soil conservation, reforestation, and roads and housing are now being vigorously pushed.

While Algeria, on the northern coast of Africa, was engaged in its long struggle for independence, a program for putting people to work and paying them with food was developed. Three hundred thousand heads of families are now receiving wages in the form of U.S. food supplemented by cash from the Algerian government. Rural rehabilitation and community development have moved forward with remarkable success.

Three agricultural counties of Algeria—Batna, Constantine, and Setis—suffered severely from the ravages of war. The countryside was seriously denuded of people through the voluntary flight of villagers to the cities. The cities were swollen with people unable to find employment and anxious to return to the country. Once home, they had to make a new start on plots that had been neglected for years and without the livestock that used to provide an important part of their subsistence. Of the three and one-half million inhabitants of the four eastern Algerian provinces two million were without any visible resources. Algeria had lost large areas of productive land through erosion—a loss accentuated by the systematic burning of massive tracts of forest land to flush out guerrilla units during the war.

Seeing this need, Church World Service in Algeria proposed that our surplus food be used to finance reforestation. It drew up plans for a program which has employed 15,500 unemployed workers on a rotation basis for two weeks out of each month. Each worker receives a daily ration to provide an adequate diet for a family of six.

Many nations around the world are experimenting with this process of using food to attack poverty and promote development through self-help projects. In the southern part of Iran, where drought has been a condition of life for centuries, where for the past five years there has been practically no rainfall, a million people live in poverty.

Virtually cut off from the more developed parts of

Iran and the rest of the world, the villagers know little about sanitation or hygiene. Many people survive by eating grass, locusts, and other insects. Vegetables are practically nonexistent. Medical services, teachers, and agricultural extension are blocked out not only by the poverty of the people but also by their inaccessibility because of the lack of roads. There is little incentive to the farmers to improve their production, since markets are beyond reach. Into this seemingly hopeless condition of life, Food for Peace has been introduced by CARE.

Following the food-for-wages experience of North Africa, CARE has devised a plan to put the people to work revitalizing their communities. The first task undertaken is a network of roads connecting the oases of the region with the sea. These roads will restore the old caravan routes of a thousand years ago by which the goods and precious treasures from Samarkand and Kabul were brought to western Europe. Working with the Iranian Red Lion and Sun Society, the Iranian equivalent of the Red Cross, CARE is bartering thirty-eight million pounds of American food abundance for an initial seventy-five-mile road. Two labor gangs of two thousand farmers, working in alternate months, receive an eight-week family ration for each four weeks of work. Rations consist of flour, cooking oil, and powdered milk to supplement the native diet of dates. By 1965, the first major road will provide this stricken region with access to the outside world.

The government of Iran is now constructing an ocean

port which will be useful to the area. Nearby deposits of coal, zinc, chromite, and red oxide can be developed. There is a regional plan for the building of small dams and the digging of wells and additional roads and for investment in Persian Gulf fishing. This region with a million inhabitants is thus on the way to becoming part of the modern world.

In strife-torn South Vietnam, one of the most appealing economic development projects is gaining strength —a plan aimed at putting 100,000 farm families into the raising of pigs.

I have watched this program with special interest, because it grew out of a suggestion that I made as Food for Peace Director. The formula for the plan was devised by an Idaho farmer, Earl Brockman, who has served since 1961 as an advisor on agricultural credit and cooperatives to our aid program in Vietnam.

"It was one of those things that just happens," Brockman recalls. "Around midnight on a January evening I was in my room in Saigon, listening to the Voice of America coming in from the Philippines. George McGovern . . . Director of Food for Peace . . . was explaining how the United States could use its surplus grains to help farmers develop cooperatives around the world. Ever since I had been in Vietnam, I'd been searching for some way to activate the cooperatives in the rural villages.

"That Voice of America broadcast got me stirred up enough to sit down and write a long letter to McGovern. About a month later, I got a letter from the Food for

Peace office in Washington, saying that the plan I had outlined had a lot of merit, and that the details and specifications of the surplus farm commodity program would be sent to me."

Given a green light from AID officials, Brockman conferred with village leaders, farmers, and Vietnamese officials; then he launched a pilot program that is now spreading nationwide.

With surplus American corn, eight sacks of cement for a pigsty, and three pigs for each participating family, the people are beginning a new occupation that is bringing better nourishment and more earning power.

AID provides the cement for pigsties, and delivers the surplus feed grains it receives from the United States under the Food for Peace program to the warehouses of the National Federation of Agricultural Cooperative Associations in Saigon and three other port cities. The National Federation stores and distributes the surplus corn and other supplies to local cooperatives. It also buys pigs and sells them to the peasants. District and local cooperatives store and sell the surplus corn and other supplies to the peasants in the pig program. As of December 31, 1963, one hundred cooperatives and forty distributors in thirty of the forty provinces were in the program. The goal is 150 cooperatives by the end of 1964.

Sanitation, disease control, and feed management practices are handled under the Vietnam government, with advice from AID technicians. Vietnamese cadres have been trained for this work.

The farmers take out 8 percent loans to buy one female breeder pig and two market pigs and to pay for whatever local materials they need to complete their concrete pigsties. They buy the surplus corn on a credit basis without interest from their cooperatives, but are expected to repay when they sell their first pigs. Repayments have already started. All it costs AID is the equivalent of about six dollars per farmer to pay for the concrete.

The corn is mostly sacked in 100-pound bags, picked up by the pig-raisers at their local cooperative and trundled home in push carts. The amount is rationed to one hundred pounds per pig per month, with the limit for any one family three hundred pounds a month. This is equivalent to two-thirds of the total average feed requirement per pig per month, with the farmer expected to buy or raise the remaining feed.

For 1963 the corn was sold to the peasants at less than the going market price. The price, however, will be stepped up from year to year until it reaches the equivalent of the normal market price for similar locally produced feeds.

The program encourages the peasants to mobilize their own resources to achieve a free and self-sustaining operation. The assistance from Food for Peace is only temporary, and is provided to help them get on their own feet as quickly as possible.

Some idea of the importance of three pigs to the Vietnam villager can be gained when one understands that the average peasant family of five to six people cultivates not more than three and one-half acres. Some plots are as small as three-fourths of an acre, the largest rarely exceed eighteen acres. Formerly the main crop was rice, but now one-half of the families raising pigs have added corn, sweet potatoes, cassava, and various greens.

In the current pig program of Vietnam, any money paid by the farmers in excess of actual costs is invested in the cooperative to help build capital. By encouraging farmers to carry on their own grain-buying business, AID is stimulating a program of self-sustained village operations. These savings have been estimated to build to several millions of dollars over a three-to-five-year period. Some of the cooperatives are already making plans to invest capital in building new warehouses and installing feed mills so they can grind corn and provide mixed feeds.

Brockman has observed that as a boy on an Idaho farm he and his family "never saw more than a few hundred dollars in cash from one year to the next. Our whole family thought we had struck it rich when my dad flashed a ten-dollar bill. We raised grain and a few hogs. Each spring my father would sell a few pigs to get some ready cash. Those pigs he sold often made all the difference in how we lived."

The same thing is now happening to thousands of farm families in Vietnam.

The Vietnam program is especially important because of its emphasis on cooperative development. American farmers have benefitted enormously from their marketing, grain storage, supply, and electric cooperatives. Much the same cooperative pattern can point the way for enormously improved rural life for millions of farm families in the developing world.

An amendment to the Foreign Aid Act of 1961 offered by Senator Hubert Humphrey of Minnesota "to encourage the development and use of cooperatives" can be of great importance. Some of our American cooperatives are now assisting in the development of cooperatives overseas and are even prepared to offer membership and patronage benefits to fledgling cooperatives abroad.

The Vietnamese hog-raising experiment, and others like it, are significant too in that they point the way out of one of our Food for Peace dilemmas. While the world's most acute nutritional need is for more protein, our surplus is largely of low-protein grain. By donating grain to farmers who will convert it into high protein hogs and poultry, we have found one way around this limitation.

One of the most hopeful developments in the attack on hunger and poverty is on Cheju Island off the coast of Korea. On this island, 300,000 people subsist at the poverty level by means of agriculture and fishing. A little barley, millet, tobacco, and vegetables are raised along the sea coast. The land ownership is about two acres of land per family, and there is some grazing of livestock on the common pasturage. No attempt has been made to fertilize or improve the land in any way. Most families keep at least one hog with a very primitive form of feeding that requires twelve to eighteen months to bring a hog to slaughter weight.

The value of this practice is so marginal that the farmers have been reluctant to set aside any grain for feeding livestock. As a result they have been unable to provide adequate nutrition for their families.

But an imaginative new Food for Peace plan proposed by Catholic Relief Services calls for the creation of a community "pig bank" to improve the quality and amount of hog production. The natives will eventually develop land for feed grain production while grants of United States feed grain permit the immediate launching of hog-raising on a rather large scale. Participating farmers will contribute half of the first litter of hogs to the community "pig bank" to assist other farmers coming into the program.

In Korea three of our voluntary agencies, CARE, Church World Service, and Seventh Day Adventists are helping twenty thousand people shift from food relief to community development projects. The agencies are contributing $115,000 worth of materials and tools. In addition to constructing dams and irrigation works, Korean workers will reclaim eight thousand acres of land in partial exchange for American food.

This transfer of resources is accompanied by an important innovation in the distribution of food to the workers. There has always been a danger that if the people received more food than they could immediately consume they would sell it in the black markets, although such sales are strictly forbidden. This problem is especially prevalent in areas where workers are seasonally employed on the development projects and then return to their farms in planting and harvest time. On this Korean project, food will be distributed to meet the workers' needs with the remaining portion of the food due credited at the provincial warehouses for later use. In this way, the workers will receive food even when they have left the project and have gone back to the tilling of their fields. The concept of saving is advanced to this extent and the food payments are adjusted to the "rural rhythm."

A sizable volume of U.S. economic aid to the Republic of China on Taiwan (Formosa) has enabled this nation to achieve an economic growth rate of approximately 6 percent a year. Real personal incomes have increased about 4 percent a year. One result is that in the near future Taiwan will follow the example of Japan and become one of the commercial purchasers of American grains and other foods.

The food imports of Taiwan constitute only 9 percent of the total consumption at present since the farmers of Taiwan are able to produce about 90 percent of the requirements. The per capita consumption has been raised to 2,400 calories a day, which is good for that area. Through the food-for-wages formula, employment has been provided to workers on fifty-eight projects requiring a total of 18.4 million man-days of labor. These projects have greatly strengthened land reclamation and soil conservation and the construction of roads, bridges, and small fishing harbors. It is unlikely that this form of economic development will be used very extensively in the future because the economy of Taiwan is highly monetized, and it seems simpler and more efficient to sell the food and pay cash wages rather than to pay partly in food. This may be a development that other nations will experience after a few years as they leave behind them some of their more primitive agricultural characteristics.

In Hong Kong, CARE is managing a hog production program making feed grain abundance available to hog producers' associations. These groups not only receive the feed grains but also technical assistance in production and marketing. The members are eligible to purchase feed and other supplies from the association at reduced prices for three years. Gradually, as they develop capital through sales of food, the prices of the feed will be increased to normal commercial rates. A capital reserve for the association will be established in the process. This group of producers may very likely become a commercial market for U.S. feed grains in the future.

Another feed grain proposal is being developed for the Philippine Islands by Xavier University College of Agriculture. The American feed grains will be used to improve the living conditions of seven hundred farm families in the Cagayan de Oro district. Santa Lucia farmers are participating in a program to upgrade local pork production with the advantage of U.S. corn surplus. In return for our feed grains, 50 percent of the pig litters are passed over to other farmers in a cooperative effort to increase food supplies and improve farming practices.

In the little African nation, Dahomey, a food-for-work program is underway to give unemployed youth roaming the streets a chance to volunteer for work in the country, clearing land and planting crops. Since Dahomey is largely deforested, the government has organized youth camps, similar to our American CCC effort of the 1930's, to plant teakwood and cashew trees.

In Dahomey, as in nearly all of the less-developed countries, people from the rural areas have been flooding into the cities hoping for employment that they seldom find. The rate of economic development is not great enough to absorb these migrants to the cities. Through food-for-work programs, however, they are being given the opportunity to work on basic civic and development projects such as road-making and simple school construction.

In all of these many ways, we are not only making more and better food available to hungry people; we are also integrating our food and feed grain into constructive self-help development programs designed to help the participants become self-sustaining. Using our food abundance to create capital through food-for-work can be exceedingly important to all of the developing nations. They desperately need roads, schools, dams, and other facilities now being constructed. That is a basic kind of capital which is necessary for all economic development. It is the equivalent of railroads in our own economic history, which opened up resources and land that made later investment profitable. The railroads first opened up our own continent to development and then provided the American farmer with profitable grain markets in Europe. It is hoped that the facilities and programs now being built with our food in the developing nations will likewise open up new opportunities for capital investment and for international trade.

Throughout most of the developing nations this program of using American food abundance to create capital is growing steadily. The program could grow more rapidly, but its growth is dependent not simply on our food supplies but also on the funds that the developing nations can make available for the cash part of the wages, for tools and equipment.

The successful expansion of the programs also depends on the quality, dedication, and care of our American AID and voluntary agency personnel. Challenging ideas and even good blueprints break down without painstaking field work, careful estimates of capabilities, local government cooperation, and close supervision. These were the qualities which U.S. AID Technician Howell Williams brought to the Tunisian "battle against underdevelopment" and that is largely why the program worked. That kind of skill and brains and dedication plus local government cooperation will bring similar results elsewhere.

The program represents a new development on the long battle line where we are skirmishing against poverty and hunger.

Perhaps of equal importance is the opportunity our food is giving the people in many developing areas to work together and to manage their own affairs. Through cooperative efforts in many small communities they are beginning to lay the foundations of a working democracy. As they become more resourceful and independent, they can be expected to place a higher value on freedom.

CHAPTER V

Alianza para el Progreso

"The Alianza para el Progreso has taken a giant leap forward. In terms of where it has to go, it has taken only a short, faltering step."
— Senator Hubert H. Humphrey, 1963

ON a chilly late afternoon, March 13, 1961, President Kennedy stood in the historic dining room of the White House before an overflow audience of Latin American diplomats and U.S. government officials. "I have called on all the people of the Hemisphere," he said, "to join in a new Alliance for Progress—Alianza para el Progreso —a vast cooperative effort, unparalleled in magnitude and nobility of purpose, to satisfy the basic needs of the American people for homes, work and land, health and schools."

As a witness to that initial ceremony and some of the subsequent chain of events, I have concluded that no other international interest gripped President Kennedy's heart and mind quite so keenly as the Alliance for Progress. He saw the problems and opportunities of our neighbors to the south with a special sense of urgency. Nor is this compelling interest difficult to understand, for Latin America is, as one observer put it, "dynamite on our doorstep."

Two weeks after his inauguration President Kennedy dispatched Special Assistant Arthur Schlesinger, Jr., and me on a mission to Latin America which took us into northeast Brazil. In this benighted section of the largest and most populous nation of Latin America our mission came face to face with the real challenge to the hemisphere. There we saw the wretched life of Brazil's twenty-seven million peasants who are trying to survive in the feudal, drought-stricken sections of the northeast. There we saw the miserable mud huts, the total absence of sanitation facilities, the villages devoid of doctors, teachers, and adequate water and food.

We saw, too, Fidel Castro's counterpart and alter ego, Francisco Juliao, the flaming peasant leader, urging his wretched followers to seize the land and destroy the suppressors.

The 215,000,000 people of Latin America occupy a vast land, potentially rich and fruitful but actually beset by misery, sickness, injustice, illiteracy, malnutrition, and misrule. It is a continent cursed by a social system that concentrates enormous wealth in the hands of the few and consigns the many to lives of desperate poverty. But powerful social forces are stirring to the south of us. Latin America is in a state of ferment fused to the following conditions:

• Two percent of the people of the continent own more than half of all its wealth and land, while most of the remainder live in hopeless poverty.

- Eighty percent of the people dwell in miserable shacks or huts.
- Illiteracy grips well over half the population.
- More than 50 percent of the people suffer from hunger and disease and most of them will never in their lifetimes see a doctor, nurse, dentist, or pharmacist.
- Most of the peasants live under primitive feudal conditions with no hope for land ownership, reasonable credit, or escape to a better life.
- Several key countries depend on one-crop economies afflicted by depressed commodity prices.
- Most governments are weakened by unjust tax structures, excessive military budgets designed to keep the government in power, bad land ownership and utilization, and indifference to shocking social problems.
- A population growth rate several times faster than the production of goods and services in several countries. With population growth already outstripping food production, Latin America's 215,000,000 population is expected to zoom to 600,000,000 by the end of the century—thirty-six years hence.

These are the target conditions which the Alliance for Progress seeks to attack. This will have to be accomplished primarily by the people of Latin America and their governments. But we can assist by the kind of cooperative efforts in funds, technical assistance, and food which President Kennedy offered.

Toward that end we have pledged our assistance at the rate of half a billion dollars a year for a decade, in the words of President Kennedy, "to combat illiteracy, improve the productivity and use of their land, wipe out disease, attack archaic tax and land-tenure structures, provide educational opportunities, and offer a broad range of projects designed to make the benefits of increasing abundance available to all."

The American contribution to the Alliance is geared to encourage self-help reform and development projects largely financed and manned by Latin Americans. We seek to stimulate a more effective use of the rich resources which the continent possesses.

If one were to ask which of those resources is the most valuable and the most significant for the future, he would get a variety of answers. Oil or minerals? Land or water? Agriculture or commerce? Any one of these is a valuable resource and needs to be more fully developed.

But the most important resource of Latin America or of any continent and the one which holds the key to the future is the children. Unless the children of Latin America can develop into healthy, educated citizens, the Alliance for Progress will amount to very little. That is why the expanding Food for Peace program has been focusing more and more on the child-feeding programs. No part of the many Alliance for Progress efforts is more important.

On May 12, 1961, Prime Minister Pedro Beltran of Peru came to my office to sign a school lunch agreement for thirty thousand Peruvian children in the poverty-stricken Puno area. That event marked the beginning of a sharpened emphasis on U.S.-assisted school feeding programs. Today, twelve million school children across the Latin American continent—one out of three children of school age—are being fed a Food for Peace lunch every day.

In the Puno section of Peru, illiteracy was 90 percent; and the learning process exceedingly slow. But teachers discovered that within six months after the school lunch program started in the fall of 1961, school attendance jumped by 40 percent and the learning capacity of the students increased sharply. Physically, the students added needed weight and strength.

Previously the children were simply too weak and listless to sit through hours of class instruction. In some areas, nine out of ten students dropped out of school before completing the sixth year. Even these brief years were marked by a lethargy that was not conducive to learning.

Little wonder then that the people of Peru have been greatly impressed by the exciting educational results of the Food for Peace school lunch effort. This program, known in Peru as the National School Nutrition Plan, which fed thirty thousand students in October 1961, had two years later jumped to 300,000 students in the primary schools. At the end of 1965, it is hoped that a million Peruvian school children will be benefitting from the program. The government of Peru is financing a large part of the cost through the construction of dining rooms and the provision of food-handling and distribution. Forty-five U.S. Peace Corpsmen are helping administer the program and offering instruction in hygiene and nutrition. Also assisting are both Catholic and Protestant religious groups who have offered their services to the government.

One of the most encouraging features is the eager participation of the parents in preparing and serving the food. They also often contribute local vegetables and bits of meat, as well as fuel.

The most exciting aspect of the program in Peru is its promise rather than its present size. Across the country in those areas not presently receiving school lunches, parents have learned about the program and are eager to see their children do as well.

The Peruvian School Nutrition Plan embodies the Alliance for Progress at its best. It calls for the sharing of resources by two cooperating governments, the close collaboration of parents and teachers, the participation of religious and benevolent groups who are assisting in the execution of the program and a combination of humane feeding with long-range human development.

"I think," said Prime Minister Beltran on signing the initial school lunch agreement, "it is clearly the beginning of what we should do in every respect, not only by cooperating in every regard to help the poor people but also to raise the standard of living of this hemisphere."

The success of the Peruvian school lunch played a major part in the decisions of the United States to initiate "Operation Niños" (operation children) in the summer of 1962. This Food for Peace effort launched within the scope of the Alliance for Progress is designed not only to accelerate the number of children being fed, but also to increase the effectiveness of the food programs through training and education.

When Operation Niños began in mid-1962, four million Latin American children were being fed through Food for Peace. At the end of 1964, that number will stand at twelve million. The program involves the close cooperation of all the governments of the hemisphere and U.S. benevolent agencies and several U.S. trade associations such as Great Plains Wheat and the American Dry Milk Institute, as well. It involves, too, such diverse groups as the Peace Corps, the American School Food Service Association, and Latin American mothers' clubs, teachers, parents, and community leaders.

Operation Niños workshops and mobile food demonstration units have been developed to increase the knowledge of nutrition, sanitation, and mass feeding. Educational booklets on the feeding of preschool children are being widely distributed through the schools. School gardens are also being developed to provide additional food.

An estimated 150,000 schools are participating in the feeding program. Brazil now has a program embracing five million children while Mexico, with one of the best school lunch programs in the world, is now feeding two million students. Food for Peace and the government of Mexico are feeding, in addition, 350,000 infants and mothers participating in the Mexican Maternal and Child Health Program.

All the countries of Latin America are now participat-

A nutrition expert explains the value of various local foods to a meeting of village women in India. The Indian Government, the U.N., the U.S., and many volunteer agencies support such programs as this.

Students at the Oriental Boat Mission School in Hong Kong. The Mennonite Church agency prepares these meals from food stocks donated by Food for Peace and the Canadian government.

Operation Niños assures these Bolivian children at least one nourishing meal a day through food donated by the U.S. AID programs (Alianza para el Progreso).

Hong Kong children receiving food from a Church World Service canteen. The CWS is one of many voluntary participants in the Food for Peace program.

ing in Operation Niños. With twelve million children receiving at least a glass of milk, and many of them a full meal, every day, we are now reaching one out of every three school age youngsters on the continent. Thus U.S. food is giving dramatic, tangible demonstration of the Alliance for Progress in the little villages and the remote rural areas, as well as in the towns and cities.

It is a form of foreign assistance which the recipient can readily grasp and understand. Sometimes the impact of our overseas aid is not apparent to the ordinary citizen in the receiving country. He is not aware of the large loans or grants of American dollars for budget support. But he has no difficulty comprehending the meaning of a glass of American milk or a roll clutched in his child's hand.

It is a memorable experience to watch the satisfaction on the faces of parents visiting their children at lunchtime in one of the new school feeding programs. As Richard Reuter puts it, "Many a father will send a child to school in order to get the food ration even if the child has to take an education along with it!"

It gives one a mingled feeling of joy and sadness, however, to note the bright, healthy faces of the children who have benefitted from a good school lunch program and then note the neglected, forlorn faces of the undernourished parents. One can only be thankful that at least we are helping to build a better and healthier future for the young. It is now estimated that of all the millions of people who are being fed through

Food for Peace worldwide, three-fourths are fifteen years of age or younger. What adult would question that priority?

American food is also supporting the Alliance for Progress as an economic development tool. In Mexico the Community Development Foundation and the Ministry of Health are using U.S. grants of food to pay part of the wages of 150,000 workers. Drawn largely from the villages where employment is frequently slack, the "people's peace corps" is digging wells, constructing reservoirs and roads, and building houses, schools, and village markets. Stress is laid on those projects which the villagers most wish to undertake.

In Bolivia, most of the Andean Indians living in the Altiplano have only a one-room hut which they share with their sheep. They do not eat the sheep, but regard them as social security to be sold only to provide funds in the event of a family illness or emergency. A diet of barley and dried potatoes gives the people between 700 and 1,100 calories daily. Cocoa leaves are chewed to suppress hunger.

One of the most impoverished nations of Latin America, Bolivia has been assisted in its development projects through local currencies generated under our Food for Peace program. Our former Ambassador to Bolivia, Ben Stephansky, has pointed out that "this form of generating funds is particularly essential in Bolivia, where widespread poverty and an abysmally low per capita national income greatly restrict the amount of money that can be obtained from taxation."

The food-for-wages formula has been used to stimulate a number of worthwhile projects in that country. The Bolivian army, for example, is now assisting in the construction of rural schools. In each case, eight or ten soldiers have joined with a group of from thirty to seventy-five villagers for the construction work. Since the villagers give their own time at considerable cost to the tilling of their fields, they receive modest quantities of Food for Peace help to offset their loss.

On the shore of Lake Titicaca more than twelve thousand feet high in the mountains of Bolivia, thirty little children are now attending a school built by their fathers, Bolivian soldiers, and American food. An adobe brick structure of one classroom, a bedroom, and cooking facilities for the teacher, it displays the Alliance for Progress plaque symbolizing the cooperative effort of twenty countries in the Western Hemisphere. Its walls consist of bricks made from mud and straw. The floor is made from rocks cut by hand and evenly spread. The ten Bolivian soldiers and the thirty *campesinos* who built the school were paid in American beans, flour, dried milk, and cornmeal.

One of the most striking examples of how food is being used to achieve important social and economic objectives is the Alto-Beni Colonization Project in Bolivia. It will be the vehicle for transferring some six thousand farm families from the cold and barren Altiplano region to highly fertile semitropical lands in the north-central section of the country. It has required penetration roads, and these are being constructed in

part by the Bolivian army and in part by the future
colonists. Soldiers and colonists who provide the manual
labor receive supplementary rations from Food for
Peace. Regular army rations are not sufficiently nourishing for such strenuous labor.

A civilian labor contingent recruited from among
Bolivia's numerous unemployed and underemployed
youth is helping to clear the land for the colonizers.
Food for Peace compensates them. The colonizers must
devote many months to access-road construction, land-
clearing, planting, and cultivating their own lands,
before they are able to harvest their first crop. Food
for Peace not only provides them with the means to
survive during this period, but is laying the foundation
for improved agricultural production and a better life
for the most depressed. In addition, we are using Food
for Peace to help finance a wool-grading and packing
cooperative which will give the Altiplano Indians a
little more income as well as a better diet.

In Brazil our food is assisting the Pindorama Colonization Cooperative—in operation for several years in
the miserable, famine-cursed northeast. The cooperative is to establish five community centers where food
will be issued to settlers during the period of land-
clearing, planting, and harvesting. The repayment for
these foodstuffs will enable the cooperatives to supply
other settlers with help. American foodstuffs will thus
serve as a revolving agricultural credit fund to allow
more and more colonists to become successful farmers.

Food-for-wages projects in this area have resulted in

new school construction, highways, sewerage systems, low-cost housing, and hospitals. Approximately 60 percent of the labor on these local projects is paid for in food. Bulgur wheat, the processed cereal which is more acceptable to the taste of many people than ordinary wheat cereal, is being used extensively in this area.

In the Andes Mountains along the west coast of South America the descendants of the Incas have restored an old custom known as the Minga, which called for one day a month of free labor for community projects. With the aid of some of our food abundance this custom is being revived and given a new meaning. In one mountain village in Ecuador, stone and sand deposits are being opened with hand labor for sale as road construction materials—a development which for the first time will bring the natives into the cash economy of the country.

We are also helping to build cooperatives by substituting food and feed grains for dollars as seed capital. A program to utilize feed grains to increase the production of chickens and eggs is now being developed. A market cooperative has been organized and plans have been completed for a series of training courses to teach qualified farmers improved methods of seed planting, irrigation, and contour plowing.

Also underway in Ecuador is an Alliance for Progress effort to speed the construction of community schools on the self-help principle. One-third of the cost is contributed by the national government, one-third by the local community and one-third by American aid. Food for Peace donations to the people in the community who have been contributing their labor to school construction permit a larger number of people to participate actively for a longer period of time.

In the heavily populated Cuzco area of Peru a food-for-work reforestation project is being undertaken under the sponsorship of Catholic Relief Services. It will immediately employ six hundred people who are expected to plant eucalyptus trees on 6,250 acres of non-agricultural land the first year. During the following nine years, 12,500 acres will be planted annually. In ten years, the project will be terminated and the first plantation will be ready for harvest. During the first year of output it is expected that a thousand people will be engaged in harvesting and manufacturing wood products and many more in manufacturing as the area grows. The funds developed from the cash wages and later from the money received from the project are expected to stimulate activity in community development and improvement in housing and schools.

In the Dominican Republic, our aid officials have approved a plan to assist small farmers in the production of hogs and poultry. To help meet a critical shortage of protein food, poultry farmers will be encouraged to expand their flocks to three hundred birds and small hog farmers to maintain up to twenty hogs. The plan makes American corn available to a local feed mill for use by the farmers. The farmer participants are expected to pay back the value of the feed after they have made sales of meat. It is, in effect, a revolving fund arrangement, made possible by our initial grant of feed grains.

In addition, the United States is "grub-staking" 5,500 families who are developing new farmland in the Dominican Republic. Under the supervision of the International Development Services, a nonprofit group in New York City, Food for Peace commodities will carry these farmers through the harvesting of two crops.

In many ways, Food for Peace is helping to advance the Alliance for Progress. But the problems of Latin America are so large that food can be no more than a partial answer. Technical assistance and financial aid are also vital.

There is a fourth ingredient of aid which is absolutely essential to the success of our efforts in Latin America. That is a widespread personal commitment of individual Americans and private groups.

Our neighbors south of the Rio Grande are part of our civilization and our spiritual tradition. They are now cast in the role of the poor man who must watch his children suffer from hunger and sickness while his rich neighbor across the street lives in comfort. This is a relationship which tends to produce jealousy and resentment and sometimes, even as we are offering aid, an irritating ingratitude.

But the goal of the Alliance is not gratitude and praise; rather, it seeks to create the conditions that make peaceful democratic growth possible. It seeks to replace despair with hope, stagnation with progress, and illness, illiteracy, and hunger with health, education, and food. We cannot give these conditions to our Latin American neighbors, but we assist and encourage them to help themselves—not just by food, funds, and government technicians, but by giving them a part of ourselves.

To do that successfully, we need to feel that their hunger and poverty, their convulsions and misery, are a special challenge to each of us. We will need to extend the time-honored American traditions of voluntary aid, community cooperation, and neighborliness to the villages, the city slums, and the rural areas of the continent. We will need to encourage a continuous dialogue between American businessmen, scholars, farmers, artists, engineers, religious leaders, and their counterparts in the republics to the south.

The first modest but nonetheless hopeful steps have already been taken. American religious and benevolent agencies have reached into every corner of the continent to assist in the operation of school lunch programs, maternal care centers, clinics, and rural and community development projects. Our Peace Corpsmen are cooperating closely in these and other constructive efforts. We are encouraging the development of housing cooperatives and farmers cooperatives—a development which could on a broad scale change the face of Latin America. In each case, we are involving Latin American citizens in cooperative, community-centered activities. The development of these grassroots patterns of community concern—an almost forgotten way of life prevalent in the colonial era of Latin America—is an essential condition of democratic growth.

The people of Latin America will in time become adequately fed. Undoubtedly they will one day secure an equitable system of taxation and land ownership. But self-rule will not function well unless the citizens care about each other enough to cooperate in the management of community affairs. North Americans who take for granted our many community action projects, voluntary associations, and humanitarian efforts, find it difficult to understand the lack of these institutions in Latin America.

Our voluntary agencies are stimulating our neighbors in the south to create voluntary self-help associations of their own. In the distribution of food, the operation of food-for-work projects and the child-feeding centers, more and more local parent and community associations are being built.

A number of our private trade, agricultural, and professional groups are also becoming involved in the Alliance. One of the most successful of these efforts is the Great Plains Wheat Association. Primarily a market development group, it has had the imagination and concern to identify closely in the villages and cities with nutritional education and school lunch development programs. Some of our rural cooperative leaders and business and labor leaders are also assisting the Alliance.

It would be most helpful if our many citizens groups would devote a year of concentrated study to the prob-

lems of Latin America followed by a year of exchange
visits in the hemisphere. Our citizens need to come to
a better understanding of the difficulties involved in
lifting standards of life in a semifeudal society. Latin
Americans, likewise, can profit from some of the hard
lessons we have learned in creating a modern society.
We know, for example, the advantages of private ownership of land distributed among many people. We know
also the desirability of increasing the total output of
the nation, as distinct from fighting one another for
shares of the existing pie.

The citizens of Latin America need to know that
their problems are understood and shared. Our own
civic leaders and citizens can do far more to determine
the future of this continent than they have thought
possible.

Our business and agricultural leaders are capable of
providing needed counsel in the development of reasonable credit arrangements, rural cooperatives, and better
distribution and use of land. The strengthening of the
economic and social institutions of rural life is perhaps
the most important task of the Alliance for Progress.
Gordon Alderfer of CARE has said: "If the battle
against hunger is to be won, the permanent victory will
depend in large measure on the total social and economic health of the rural, food-producing communities
throughout the hungry areas of the world."

We of course have an economic as well as a moral
and political stake in the success of these efforts to
raise standards of life. If the people of Latin America

achieve even a 2 percent annual increase in personal income, their anticipated population of 600,000,000 in the year 2000 will have a purchasing power six times what it is today. Certainly a major new demand for American agricultural and industrial goods will be one result.

The mutual aid philosophy behind the Alliance for Progress includes a number of other valuable by-products. It gives hope and encouragement to the Latin Americans and it provides a sense of constructive participation for American citizens. The importance of citizen participation in American foreign policy is underscored in a letter the author received in 1961 from a friend representing Great Plains Wheat in Peru, Harlan Parkinson, who recently suffered an untimely death. He wrote:

One of the reasons the American people have magnified the Cuban problem at the expense of diminishing the more complex problems of poverty, misery, and ignorance throughout Latin America is that they have not been given a significant opportunity to participate in the solution of these broader problems...

One of the most rewarding things about Great Plains Wheat is that we have been able to show our 300,000 midwestern wheat farmer members why it is in their interest to assist the lower classes of Latin America to obtain a better way of life.

Food for Peace gives our farmers, our voluntary agencies, our private trade and agricultural groups a stake in the Alliance for Progress.

The yawning gap between the misery of most Latin

Americans today and the ambitious goals of the Alliance will sometimes seem overwhelming. Much of the time it may appear that we are simply holding the fort rather than advancing to victory. Nor will the effort be free from turbulence and upheaval. Four democratic governments—Ecuador, Guatemala, Honduras, and the Dominican Republic—were overturned by military coups in 1963 alone. Brazil followed the same route in 1964.

The Alliance for Progress calls for a much more courageous exercise than simply cursing Castro. It seeks to replace the swamplands of hopelessness and misery which gave that dictator his opportunity. It envisions nothing less than a peaceful continentwide revolution that may require—not a decade—but a generation or more to complete.

There are those who have already grown weary in the battle. They would have us retreat. But to do so may present us and our children with a much more painful cost in the future. If rural Latin America cannot break out of the grip of feudalism and the city slums cannot be redeemed, we will tomorrow see far less hope for freedom and stability than exists today.

If we succeed, however, then we can know that this hemisphere will provide a home for prosperity, dignity, and peace.

CHAPTER VI

Food and the India Way

"Their happiness does not depend upon their being thinly or fully inhabited, upon their poverty or their richness, their youth or their age, but on the proportion which the population and the food bear to each other."
— Thomas Robert Malthus, *Essay on the Principle of Population*, 1798

WHEN famine struck the Indian province of Bengal in 1943, more than a million people died of starvation. One observer described "the rumble of trucks piled high with human bodies bound for mass graves on the outskirts of Calcutta."

Two decades after this tragic famine, I participated with the Indian Food Minister, S. K. Patil, in a dockside ceremony at Bombay marking the arrival of the 14,000,-000th ton of wheat shipped to India under the Public Law 480 Food for Peace program. That ceremony of February 7, 1962, dramatized the vital role of American food in Indian life.

Mr. Patil took this occasion to thank the people of the United States for the growing volume of wheat and rice that has flowed to India since 1951. To a cheering throng of dock workers, seamen, visitors, and government officials, he said that American grain had prevented the recurrence of massive famines of the kind that struck Bengal in 1943. He stressed that U.S. food had checked inflation, stabilized local food prices, strengthened the health and energy of the Indian people, and provided a vital reserve against natural disaster.

Three-fourths of India's 450,000,000 people are engaged in agriculture; so food imports must not be permitted to discourage local production and marketing. It was thus gratifying to hear Mr. Patil stress that far from delaying India's agricultural growth, American grain had enabled him as Food Minister to concentrate on efforts to increase domestic food production. During the last decade, he said, India had increased her grain production from fifty million to eighty million tons annually. Furthermore, with the assurance of grain supplies from the United States, two or three million tons of hoarded food had come into the market for use.

Since India gained independence, more than $4 billion in American aid has gone to that country in food, money, and technical assistance. Of that total, more than half has been food, making India by far the largest recipient of Food for Peace.

Twenty-nine million tons of wheat has been committed—most of it under the authority of Public Law 480. This is the equivalent of nearly one complete U.S. wheat crop. Combined with the 1.6 million tons of rice that Food for Peace has brought to India, it would provide 140 pounds of food for every person in the country. Two million bales of cotton—or seven yards of cloth for every Indian—has also been committed under Food for Peace.

The first American economic aid to India came with the enactment of the India Emergency Act of 1951— a loan to finance the purchase of two million tons of U.S. wheat. Although repayment of the wheat loan was to have commenced on June 30, 1957, Indian foreign exchange difficulties led the United States to reschedule repayments to begin December 31, 1986, through June 30, 1995, with no additional interest charges.

The 1951 wheat loan provided that the first $5 million of interest payments would be used to strengthen Indian institutions of higher learning. To administer this provision, the U.S. Information Service set up in 1954 the India Wheat Loan Educational Exchange Program. Interest payments at 2½ percent have now been largely expended for scientific equipment, books, and the exchange of American and Indian university professors.

In 1955, the Mutual Security Act, under which India and other nations had been receiving financial and technical aid, was amended by Congress to provide that a portion of the aid must be agricultural commodities. This channel brought $67.8 million in wheat and cotton to India with the sales proceeds used to finance technical and economic aid projects and the exchange of personnel between the two countries.

By far the largest volume of food for India has moved

through five separate agreements under Title I of Public Law 480 beginning on August 29, 1956, and concluding with the biggest grain transaction in history on May 4, 1960. The 1960 agreement provided for the shipment of sixteen million tons of wheat—587 million bushels—over a four-year period, and a million tons of rice—some twenty-two million bags. Supplements of cotton, corn, and soybeans have since been added, bringing the total transaction to $1.4 billion. The four prior agreements totaled roughly a billion dollars.

Signed at the White House by President Eisenhower and Indian Food Minister Patil, the agreement in effect committed the United States to a shipload of wheat every day for four years. This transaction was unique, not only because of its enormous size, but also because it was the first to span a four-year period. It also provided for the first time for the creation of a national food reserve with one-fourth of the wheat and all of the rice set aside by the Indian Government for this purpose.

"For a country as large as ours with a population of over 400,000,000 people and with a history of recurrent food shortages, a national food reserve is of paramount importance," said Food Minister Patil in signing the agreement. "Freed from the anxiety of food shortages we shall be able to concentrate our efforts and energies to the all-round development of our country," he said.

There can be no doubt that the four-year agreement and previous food shipments contributed enormously to India's stability and growth. They have largely put an end to mass starvation, inflation, and hoarding.

India is the classic example of a developing country. It includes the whole range of problems and opportunities, heartache, and hope which characterize much of Asia, Africa, and Latin America. By far the world's largest nation next to China, it will play a crucial role in influencing the course of Asia and the entire world.

Perhaps the greatest question facing Asia today is whether it will go "the China way" or "the India way." Will it take the path of violent revolution followed by Communist regimentation of society, or will it follow the peaceful, constitutional pattern of political and economic development?

The government and the people of India are trying to answer that question through peaceful but painstaking economic, social, and political development. They have undertaken a march into the modern world while laden with the heavy burdens of the old.

Since being granted independence in 1947 and establishing a constitutional government in January, 1950, Indians have been struggling to build a democratic society in a vast land where eighty of every one hundred people can neither read nor write.

They are striving for improved living standards through agricultural and industrial development with average personal income now $70 a year or 19 cents a day.

They are weakened by generations of hunger and neglect. Since independence their life span has in-

creased from twenty-seven to thirty-two years and
calorie intake has climbed from 1,800 to 2,100, but
chronic malnutrition continues to give India one of the
world's highest death rates and one of the lowest protein and calorie intakes. The average Indian male
weighs 106 pounds, while the women average 92
pounds. Even that inadequate weight is derived from
improperly balanced diets.

The aged cows and hordes of marauding monkeys,
regarded as sacred, aggravate India's food problem
since these animals eat large quantities of food that
could otherwise go to the people.

India is also torn by religious nationalism which
separated the Indian subcontinent into three parts at
the time of independence—India, Pakistan, and East
Pakistan. Still in dispute is the province of Kashmir—
claimed by both India and Pakistan.

Fourteen languages and many dialects deprive the
nation of a common communications medium.

The caste system inhibits the economic and social
progress of the people and scorns physical labor as im-
proper for the higher castes.

In the rural areas which embrace eighty-three of one
hundred Indians, there is a shortage of rural credit,
extension services, pesticides, fertilizer, and machinery
—all devices which have made possible the productivity
of the American farmer.

On top of all these obstacles is the rapid growth of
population, adding eight million new mouths every
year.

Yet, India is moving forward, thanks to an enlightened government, a skillful civil service—a legacy of the British—an influential though small cadre of economists and other citizens educated in Western universities, and a patient populace that seems willing to follow the path of peaceful, democratic evolution.

India is completing her third five-year plan—comprehensive efforts to lift agricultural and industrial production, develop water and power potential, reduce disease and hunger, strengthen the fabric of rural and community life, and increase education and family planning. All of these brave efforts are moving ahead, however slowly.

Since independence India has doubled school attendance and the number of medical students, added fifty thousand new hospital beds, built 1,800 family planning centers, increased grain production from fifty-two million tons annually to eighty million, started 3,100 community development projects embracing 400,000 villages and 200,000,000 people, and inaugurated thousands of Panchayat governing councils in the half million villages of the nation.

It is clear that the winning of political independence has sharpened the demand and the determination of the people of India for better standards of life—for more food and clothing, for improved education, health, and nutrition. The development plans are the result of this demand.

Paradoxically, development efforts often result in critical food shortages. Health measures, such as the eradication of malaria, and the decline of infant mortality resulting from improved sanitation, mean longer life spans. As a consequence, the Indian population, which was expected to rise at a rate of five million annually, has been going up at a pace of eight million.

Employment of large numbers of workers on development projects such as dam construction has meant more buying power which is reflected first in food purchases. The Indian Ministry of Food has estimated that between 1950 and 1956 average per capita consumption jumped by 276 calories.

These factors place a heavy demand on food supplies, leading to rising farm prices. In the absence of large supplies of American produce, the entire Indian development plan would have been crippled by a critical shortage of food accompanied by painful inflation.

Food for Peace has contributed to India's five-year development plans by securing necessary public financing for irrigation, dams, roads, schools, and other public works. In poor countries, it is not easy to secure private savings for investment in new development. Low per capita income makes it difficult to secure public funds from taxation. But the government of India has secured hundreds of millions of rupees through the sale to its people of Food for Peace commodities. In this way, the entire populace has been contributing to the success of the development plans. Purchases in the marketplace of American food have provided the finances to underwrite projects that increase agricultural and industrial production. In other words, American farmers are not only feeding hungry people, but are indirectly helping the Indians to increase their own food production.

Food grains moving to India are purchased by the India Supply Mission in Washington from American grain companies. After the best offers have been selected by the Supply Mission, the grain is inspected before shipment to determine that it meets specifications.

The only difference in these transactions from normal commercial arrangements is that no Indian foreign exchange in either dollars or gold is used. Instead, the American trader is paid by the United States Government with grain from government surplus stocks or with dollars derived from the sale of such stocks. The Indian government then agrees to deposit an equivalent amount of rupees to be expended for purposes agreed upon by the two governments. The Indian government recovers its investment in rupees when the food is sold to its consumers.

To date, America has granted to the Indian government for economic development projects one-third of the rupees received in payment for our food and cotton. Another 46 percent of the rupees has been loaned for development purposes. In other words, 80 percent of all proceeds derived from nearly $2½ billion of sales has been committed to the Indian five-year plans. Another 7 percent has been set aside as loans to private American and Indian business firms operating in India. The remaining 13 percent of the rupees has been earmarked for U.S. expenditures in India, including the financing of Fulbright scholarships, embassy expenses,

U.S. market development, and U.S. information activities. Of course, a sizable portion of the rupees loaned to the Indian government will come back to the U.S. account.

One of the most thrilling projects financed by Food for Peace is the eradication of malaria. Rupees granted to the Indian government from the sale of American wheat have helped to underwrite the cost of this remarkably successful campaign. Prior to Indian independence, malaria struck a hundred million Indians yearly with two million resulting deaths. Today, after a decade of U.S. assistance this scourge, once India's number one medical problem, has been nearly eradicated. How can one evaluate the saving of two million lives each year plus the prevention of a hundred million cases a year of this destroyer of health and energy?

At Kanpur, rupees received from the sale of American wheat have been returned to the Indian government to help finance the Indian Institute of Technology. This institution, one of four established since World War II, seeks to provide urgently needed quality engineers. Nine American universities have cooperated to provide American professors for the Institute. Also, native faculty members are receiving advanced education in the United States.

Food for Peace rupees are also helping to finance the development of fifty-five new milk supply depots in the cities across India. The ever-present protein shortage so typical of the underdeveloped country gives this effort a special importance. American dairy specialists are working closely in this development. U.S. pasteurizing, bottling, and processing equipment has also been furnished.

Most of the rupee loans have gone to irrigation and hydroelectric power development. Hundreds of thousands of Indian workers are developing the water resources of the country. One of these many projects is the great Hirakud Dam across the Mahandi River. Three miles in length, this dam is the longest in the world. It is flanked by thirteen miles of dikes on each side of the river. The enormous reservoir of water impounded by the project will irrigate 570 thousand acres of farmland in the State of Orissa and generate a quarter of a million kilowatts of hydroelectric power.

Scores of other projects—the U.P. Agricultural University, the All-India Institute of Medical Sciences, the Trombay Fertilizer Factory, National Highways, Soil Conservation, the Industrial Credit and Investment Corporation—have been financed partly by proceeds derived from Food for Peace sales.

Under the amendment to Public Law 480, named after Congressman Harold Cooley of North Carolina, up to one-fourth of the local currencies generated by Food for Peace sales may be loaned to private enterprise. Two types of borrowers are eligible: (1) U.S. businesses, their overseas subsidiaries or affiliated firms in the host country; (2) host country firms aiding the use of American farm produce such as grain storage companies or flour mills. The Goodyear Tire Company, the American Home Products Corporation, the Otis

Elevator Company, and Allis-Chalmers are a few of the companies benefiting from Cooley loans, which will be repaid at 6 percent interest.

One problem facing us with reference to the Food for Peace currencies is a considerable accumulation of unused rupees in the U.S. account. As the loan portion of our food agreements is repaid, this account will continue to grow. It is important that these currencies which go beyond U.S. uses be spent in a manner that does not exert inflationary pressures on the economy. We ought to consider the establishment of a binational foundation of distinguished American and Indian citizens with a format similar to the Ford or Rockefeller Foundation. One noninflationary project that such a foundation could undertake would be a nationwide program of family planning and information. Such a program could effectively use all of the surplus currency without stimulating inflation.

In India, as elsewhere, American food is being used directly to pay part of the wages of men working on irrigation and land reclamation projects. The government of India has tended to view the food-for-wages formula as a contradiction of its desire for a monetized economy. But there are practical reasons for using food on a much larger scale in rural and community development projects to finance wage costs. This opportunity is better appreciated when one remembers that the typical Indian villager devotes two-thirds of his income to food purchases. There are millions of underemployed village and rural Indians who ought to be working on a variety of labor-intensive projects with part of their wages paid in food. The Food for Peace economic development program should be multiplied many times over across the country.

Also, there is an urgent need for much more protein production, which U.S. feed grains and technical assistance can help supply. A combination of feed grain, proper mixing, and careful supervision can bring about desperately needed increases in the production of poultry, eggs, and milk in India. Food for Peace is engaged on a small scale in this effort, but much more can and should be accomplished. Cooperative associations of Indian farmers should be encouraged on a broad scale to lead the way in the development of vastly increased supplies of chickens, eggs, and milk. We have encouraged the establishment of several highly successful dairies. But an imaginative use of our feed grains and technical assistance can, with Indian cooperation, go much further in the production of protein foods.

Of all the food programs we have launched, none is more filled with promise for the future than the Indian school lunch and preschool feeding programs. With CARE leading the way, the voluntary agencies, including UNICEF and Catholic Relief Services, Church World Service, and Lutheran World Relief are now feeding ten million children a daily lunch—most of these in the schools.

I have visited a number of these preschool and school lunch programs and had the privilege of inaugurating a large school milk program in the Punjab in February,

1962. Indeed, one of my early actions as Food for Peace
Director was to send a message to the Indian government in April 1961 indicating U.S. willingness to participate in a sharply expanded school lunch program.
This is the phase of Food for Peace on which the most
intensive effort should be concentrated in the years
ahead. This is the way to help the children of India
develop healthy bodies, sound minds, and rudimentary
education. No more valuable contribution could be devised for the future well-being of India.

Doctors and nutritionists know that in the years after
weaning until he starts to school a child can suffer
irreparable harm to body, mind, and spirit as a result
of dietary lacks and especially protein deficiency. It is
literally beyond comprehension to consider the fantastic
economic, cultural, and spiritual loss to a vast country
such as India resulting from the lack of proper food
for little children. Tens upon tens of millions of Indian
children have been consigned to lives of listlessness,
mental retardation, and misery because their bodies
and minds were warped by malnutrition in the early
formative years.

What more practical goal could we set for Food for
Peace than to reach every child in India under school
age and every nursing and pregnant mother with a
daily feeding program. It can be done and it will pay
dividends beyond measure.

In the past decade Indian school attendance has
doubled from 25,000,000 to about 50,000,000 and is
expected to attain 64,000,000 by 1966. We are now

reaching about one pupil in five with a school lunch. The results in energy, health, learning, and spirit have been a joy to behold. Here again, I would hope that a goal would be set to offer every school child a daily lunch.

Every reasonable effort should be made to support and expand nutritional information, education, and training. Currencies generated from Title I food sales should be allocated for these purposes to assist efforts on the part of local and state governments, voluntary agencies such as CARE, and the Peace Corps.

Personnel participating in the large CARE school feeding programs are experienced and well-trained. They have an appreciation for the nutritional aspects of a carefully organized school lunch program. But there is need for many more trained Indian personnel with a good knowledge of nutrition to help as supervisors. Efforts by government and private agencies should be carefully coordinated in a sustained nutritional campaign to include every elementary and secondary student in the country.

When one considers the inexhaustible needs of India's 450,000,000 people for housing, medical care, sanitation, and adequate income, the prospect is almost overwhelming. But, it is not overwhelming and not unreasonable to bring Food for Peace into every classroom, and establish some kind of preschool and maternal feeding arrangement in every village in India.

If that task is accomplished, the India way will more likely be the wave of the future in Asia.

CHAPTER VII

Freedom from Hunger

"We desire to state with all the emphasis at our command that freedom from hunger is man's first fundamental right."
—Special Assembly, Food and Agriculture Organization,
Rome, March 14, 1963

ON March 30, 1943, at the peak of World War II, President Franklin D. Roosevelt issued invitations to the countries associated with the United States in the war to meet in conference on the problems of agriculture and nutrition at Hot Springs, Virginia. In session from May 18 to June 3, 1943, this conference was the forerunner of other United Nations activities formally launched two years later.

President Roosevelt called the conference to stimulate an exchange of views on steps that could be taken in the postwar world to strengthen the agricultural economies of the nations and improve nutritional conditions throughout the world. Marvin Jones, chairman of the United States delegation, was elected president of the conference, attended by delegates from forty-four nations.

This first World Food Congress established an interim commission with an office in Washington, D.C., which functioned until the Food and Agriculture Organization (FAO) was formally created at Quebec on October 16, 1945. The representatives of thirty-four nations signing the United Nations FAO Constitution at Quebec pledged their nations to individual and collective efforts to improve nutritional standards, elevate rural living conditions, and increase the effective production and distribution of food. Nearly all of the nations now members of the United Nations have also become affiliated with the Food and Agriculture Organization. Its headquarters was transferred from Washington to Rome early in 1951.

FAO is governed by a conference composed of one voting delegate from each member state which meets in biennial sessions. A Council of twenty-five member governments designated by the conference serves as the governing body between sessions. Most of the work assigned to the council is actually done by standing committees.

The programs and activities of FAO are planned and executed by a full-time Director-General, currently Dr. B. R. Sen of India, and a secretariat of several hundred technical experts, consultants, and administrative personnel.

FAO cooperates closely with the United Nations Special Fund and such other UN agencies as the Children's Fund and the World Health Organization. It

derives operating funds, as does the regular United
Nations organization, from the member nations.

During two decades of operation, FAO has provided
the opportunity for consultation between nations on
the complex problems of food production, distribution,
and trade. It has published a large volume of informational materials and offered valuable technical assistance
to developing countries in all parts of the world.

In its early years FAO depended largely on the
technical mission of a few months' duration designed to
complete a survey and propose guidelines of development for a particular country or region. In more recent
years, it has concentrated on special projects to which
it has assigned experts for a period of a year or more.
The FAO technicians remain long enough to lay the
groundwork for an irrigation unit, a training institute,
a pest control program, or a livestock management
project.

Perhaps the most fundamental contribution of FAO
is an enlargement of international cooperation in the
all-important fields of food and agriculture. Nations
have learned through the conferences, missions, research, publications, and field projects of FAO that
they can assist each other greatly by working together.

The first Director-General of the organization, Lord
Boyd Orr of Scotland, who won a Nobel Prize for his
efforts, envisioned a World Food Bank designed to
funnel food surpluses to areas of hunger. In this way the
farmers would be protected against the price-depress-
ing effect of their surpluses while countries with food

shortages would be protected against hunger. The World Food Bank scheme developed considerable support in the United States and elsewhere but was blocked largely by fears that it would disrupt normal commercial markets and farm prices.

In July of 1960, FAO, with the approval and cooperation of the United Nations system, launched the five-year worldwide Freedom from Hunger Campaign. The proposal was first submitted two years earlier to the Economic and Social Council of the United Nations by Director-General B. R. Sen. It seeks to focus public attention on the challenge of hunger. The basic thrust of the campaign is not the feeding of hungry people with farm surpluses from abroad; rather, it seeks to encourage the capacity of the developing countries to meet their own needs. It has undertaken a large-scale information and education effort to acquaint governments and citizens with the facts of hunger and methods of improved food production.

The message to the more affluent nations has concentrated on arousing public awareness of the danger which global hunger and malnutrition pose to the peace and progress of mankind. It has sought also to encourage international cooperation in facing up to the solution of these problems. To the poorer countries the campaign message has sought to stimulate the confidence that a vigorous national effort, aided by more fortunate nations, can break the bonds of hunger.

Every nation has been urged to establish a Citizens' Freedom from Hunger Foundation to raise funds for the campaign. In this fashion private individuals, women's clubs, religious groups, civic organizations, and commercial firms can participate through contributions of money or materials.

The American Freedom from Hunger Foundation Campaign was named by President Kennedy on November 22, 1961, the day before Thanksgiving. Mr. Kennedy participated with me in a simple ceremony in the Fish Room of the White House to launch the U.S. phase of the campaign. Representing the new foundation were Mrs. Woodrow Wilson, widow of the President, and Miss Marian Anderson, the great Negro singer. Chancellor Konrad Adenauer of the West German Republic, who was at the White House for a discussion with the President, accepted Mr. Kennedy's invitation to join in the ceremony. This was Mrs. Wilson's last public appearance prior to her death.

The American Foundation was headed first by Alvin Shapiro of Washington, D.C., a maritime official; then by James Patton, a long-time leading advocate of Food for Peace and president of the National Farmers Union. The present head of the foundation is Herbert Sugden of the Virgin Islands. Robert Nathan, Washington economist, has played an important role in sparking the U. S. Freedom from Hunger Foundation.

A campaign trust fund administered by the Director-General of FAO will receive and disburse contributions to finance informational, research, and selected action projects.

The Freedom from Hunger Campaign in its opening

Tunisian laborers working under the food-for-wages program assist in the construction of low-cost housing.

Indian laborers fill bags with food grains shipped from the United States under Public Law 480.

The launching of the Freedom from Hunger Campaign at the White House, Nov. 22, 1961. From left to right: Marian Anderson, Senator McGovern, President Kennedy, Chancellor Adenauer, and Mrs. Woodrow Wilson.

Senator McGovern and President Johnson discuss the future of the Food for Peace program.

years was centered largely on public information, but its second half has been concentrated more on projects designed to improve rural living in the less-developed nations. For example, the fertilizer industries of the United States and several other countries are cooperating in a program that has made $2 million in cash and fertilizer available to poor countries. More than eleven thousand fertilizer demonstrations have been executed in various parts of the world.

The people of the Netherlands are financing another Freedom from Hunger campaign project in the Near East. They have donated $110,000 to train young farmers in that region and to purchase seeds and equipment.

The Evangelical Churches of Western Germany are financing a project in Northern Nigeria to develop crops of beans, peas, and lentils to offset a critical protein shortage. A second project supported by the German churches is developing rice production in the vast unused swamplands of Liberia.

In several countries in East Africa, agricultural colleges have been established at an average cost of $50,000 to $150,000, financed by the United Kingdom Committee. School gardens and nutritional education in the Sudan, at a cost of $125,000, have been financed by the Canadian Freedom from Hunger Committee. The Netherlands committee has financed home gardens in Dahomey and Sierra Leone at a cost of nearly $400,-000. A veterinary training center in Sweden costing $72,000 has been financed by the Swedish Freedom from Hunger Campaign. A plant pest-control training center in Southeast Asia, at a cost of $150,000, has been financed by the Australian Freedom from Hunger Committee.

Dozens of similar projects approved by the campaign staff and financed by private groups around the world are now moving ahead.

A highlight of the campaign was the World Food Congress in Washington, D.C., June 4-18, 1963, timed to commemorate the twentieth anniversary of the Hot Springs World Food Conference. Statesmen, scientists, religious leaders, nutritionists, farm leaders, industrial experts, and a host of citizens from all parts of the world converged on Washington for two weeks of intensive discussion of all aspects of world food problems.

President Kennedy opened the congress with the declaration: "So long as freedom from hunger is only half-achieved . . . no citizen, no nation can afford to feel satisfied or secure. We have the ability, we have the means, and we have the capacity to eliminate hunger from the face of the earth. We need only the will."

The congress concluded with an address by Director Sen in which he asserted that "agricultural development must be the cornerstone of economic growth." More fertilizer, better seeds, pesticides, irrigation, farm implements, rural education, extension services, farmers cooperatives, more equitable land ownership, improved nutrition, and assistance from the more fortunate nations—these are the tools that the congress spotlighted as the way to freedom from hunger.

Operating within the framework of the Freedom from

Hunger Campaign and, indeed, providing its most concrete feature is the experimental World Food Program. It is the outgrowth of a resolution of October 27, 1960, passed by the General Assembly of the United Nations —the Resolution for the Provision of Food Surpluses to Food-Deficient Peoples through the United Nations System.

The UN resolution called on the FAO to establish procedures by which food surpluses could be used in a manner compatible with the economic development of the food-deficit countries. Toward this end the Director-General of FAO was asked to prepare a report.

In early April, 1961, Dr. Sen, with the aid of a group of experts, presented his report to a small intergovernmental advisory committee of FAO member states meeting in Rome. As an American delegate to this session, I decided after consultations in Rome with my fellow delegates, Mr. Raymond Ioanes of the Department of Agriculture and Mr. Sidney Jacques of the State Department, that while the report by Dr. Sen was excellent, it needed a concrete proposal to make it meaningful.

We therefore made a transatlantic telephone call requesting clearance by the White House and the Departments of State and Agriculture to make an offer on behalf of the United States toward an initial world food program. We suggested a beginning effort of $100 million in farm commodities and cash, with the United States pledging $40 million in commodities and exploring with Congress the possibility of $10 million in cash.

Within twenty-four hours we were authorized by

Washington to suggest such a proposal to the Director-General and the advisory committee in Rome. The statement, offered on April 10, 1961, one of the shortest made during the week-long session, was as follows:

1. The United States favors a multilateral approach for the use of agricultural commodities as a supplement to bilateral arrangements.

2. We think FAO should have a major role in such a program, in cooperation with other UN organizations.

3. We believe this should be a truly multilateral program with the widest possible contribution by member countries.

4. We recognize that countries are here to advise the Director-General on his report—not to take government positions on subjects covered in his report. Because of the need to move to the consideration of specific action proposals, however, we have been in touch with our Government over the weekend.

5. As a result, we are authorized to propose that an initial program on a multilateral basis might aim at a fund of $100 million in commodities and cash contributions. For its part, the United States would be prepared to offer $40 million in commodities, and the possibility of a supplementary cash contribution will be explored in Washington.

6. The $100 million total would be available for use over a fixed forward period. We are thinking of three years.

7. We recognize the desire of the Director-General

to make the widest possible use of commodities in alleviating malnutrition. However, we continue to believe that the primary aim of the program in its initial stage should be to meet emergency needs. At the same time, we would support use of the program fund for pilot activities in other fields such as school lunch or labor-intensive projects, in order to develop some diversified experience.

8. Specifics including additional staffing would have to be worked out for consideration by governments. This could be the responsibility of the Director-General in informal consultation with individual countries.

9. The purpose of our proposal is to help in launching a multilateral program utilizing food and to test approaches. After such experience, we could then examine the question of future additional work.

Resolutions by the FAO and the United Nations at the end of 1961 and early in 1962 approved the World Food Program in substantially the form outlined in the April 1961 proposal in Rome. The program is now jointly governed by the United Nations and the FAO through a twenty-nation Intergovernmental Committee. An executive director, Mr. A. H. Boerma of the Netherlands, and a small secretariat direct the effort from FAO headquarters in Rome. Forty nations have voluntarily contributed to the $100 million in commodities, cash, and shipping that will capitalize the three-year experiment.

During the late fall of 1961, before the proposal was realized, a brief but intense behind-the-scenes dispute developed between State Department officials and our representatives to the United Nations in New York. The State Department generally favored a limited experimental plan along the lines suggested at Rome. Some of our UN representatives, however, favored a much larger allocation of U. S. surpluses to be administered through the UN Special Fund in New York. Although the issue was resolved on the side of the Rome proposal, if this experiment is successful, it should encourage rather than foreclose a larger United Nations effort in the future.

The World Food Program is experimenting over a three-year period, 1963-1965, with three types of food utilization: economic development projects, child feeding, and emergency needs.

The economic development projects include the temporary provision of food to migrant farm families who need to devote their full labor to cultivating newly occupied land. Such assistance can also be helpful to ease the dislocations that result from land reform.

Feed grains are being used to promote livestock and poultry production through the introduction of more balanced mixed feeds.

Food is also being used to finance some of the wage costs involved in community road, hospital, housing, and school construction.

In some instances food aid is used as a buffer supply to prevent painful fluctuations of local market prices.

The child-feeding programs are in a different mold from the economic development projects, but they contribute both to human health and community development. The World Food Program is seeking to improve the diets of all pregnant mothers and young children in a specified area. It utilizes community development projects and maternal centers in cooperation with UNICEF and the World Health Organization. The school feeding programs are concentrating on testing the impact of daily lunches on school attendance and health.

The emergency program is based on a modest pool of foodstuffs which can be rushed to areas experiencing a flood, drought, earthquake, or other catastrophe.

The World Food Program is admittedly small—only $100 million in commodities and cash for a three-year period, compared to the $2 billion annual outlay of Food for Peace. But it is large enough to test the strengths and weaknesses of using food surpluses constructively on a multilateral basis. It may point the way to much larger cooperative efforts by the nations of the world.

The great strength of the Freedom from Hunger Campaign and the World Food Program is that they seek to abolish hunger, not by ministering temporarily to longer breadlines, but by permanently improving food production in the developing countries through international cooperation.

It will take this kind of global effort to avert otherwise certain starvation for multitudes of mankind. The population of 1980 will call for a doubling of present food production; by the year 2000 food output must be tripled. These statistics may be the most important facts in the world we are creating for our children.

In launching the Freedom from Hunger Campaign in July of 1960, Dr. Sen said: "One man's hunger and want is every man's hunger and want. One man's freedom from hunger and want is neither a true nor a secure freedom until all men are free from hunger and want."

If men everywhere grasp the full meaning of that statement, freedom from hunger will be achieved in our time.

CHAPTER VIII

Victory in the War Against Want

"Any man and any nation that seeks peace and hates war and is willing to fight the good fight against hunger . . . will find the United States of America by their side, willing to walk every step of the way."
—President Lyndon B. Johnson, United Nations Address,
December 17, 1963

"IT is going to be a first-class crime if anyone in this world lacks food in another decade."

So writes Jonathan Garst, brother of Roswell Garst, the Coon Rapids, Iowa, farmer who was Nikita Khrushchev's host on his first visit to the United States.

Having maintained a lively intellectual and practical interest in the progress of agriculture for half a century, the Garst brothers symbolize the revolutionary changes that have made the American farmer the envy of the world.

Some Americans were surprised that Khrushchev would devote two days' time to a farm in Coon Rapids, considering all the attractions America has to offer a visitor on his first look at our country. But this decision is simply explained. Mr. Khrushchev is a hard-headed realist who knows that agriculture has been the weakest link in the Soviet economy. For years he has been searching for formulas to accelerate the unsatisfactory food production of his country. No other domestic subject seems to have claimed so much of his interest, energy, and concern.

Khrushchev knows that nearly half of the entire Russian labor force is tied to the land in producing food. In the United States only 8 percent of our manpower is devoted to agriculture. Yet, the remaining 92 percent is better fed than is the Russian populace. Furthermore, while Russia's vast farm population has been unable even to feed the other half of the nation, American food is flowing into every corner of the globe.

Mr. Khrushchev is too wise to miss the enormous advantage which this condition gives to the United States. Our agricultural efficiency releases millions of men for production in industry. It gives us a major source of foreign exchange—more than from any other industry. It places a powerful foreign policy tool in our hands at a time when hungry nations are hanging in the balance of world politics.

Mr. Khrushchev knows that a few short years after the United States developed nuclear bombs, his scientists were able to duplicate this feat. He knows that his engineers and scientists launched the first space satellite, Sputnik I. He knows that the biggest hydroelectric dam in the world is in the Soviet Union. But he also knows that both Russian and Chinese Communist planners have fallen down on the farm—a spec-

tacle which led Walt Rostow to observe some years ago
that "Marx was a city boy."

And so Mr. Khrushchev came to Coon Rapids to see
and to learn for himself.

The Garst family began operating the farm at Coon
Rapids in 1915. At that time, one out of three Americans
lived on farms. Today the ratio is one out of twelve.
In 1915 the Garsts ran their 200-acre farm with the aid
of a few simple horse-drawn implements. The farmhouse was lighted by a kerosene lantern and there were
few labor-saving devices for either the farmer or his
wife. No tractors, mechanical corn-pickers, or combines
had yet been developed. Indeed, as Jonathan Garst puts
it, "Thomas Jefferson would have felt very much at
home on the farm at Coon Rapids."

The great changes in American agriculture came at
an accelerating pace after 1915 with the sharply increased demands for food of World War I serving as
a catalyst. In the half century since then the American
farm has been transformed. Every phase of the farm
operation is heavily assisted by machinery. Rural elec-
trification not only lights the farmhouse but runs every-
thing from the water pump to the milking machine.
Hybrid seed, chemical fertilizer, pesticides, livestock
feed supplements, soybean products, and a host of other
developments, including the cooperative movement,
have changed the face and the form of rural America.

Three historic acts of 1862—the Homestead Act, the
Morrill Act, and the creation of the Department of

Agriculture—had long before laid the institutional foundation of American agriculture.

The Homestead Act established the pattern of individual family farm ownership and operation which is the heart of rural America and the key to our amazing production. Farming is such demanding toil that it requires the labor of an interested owner for maximum results. The Homestead Act opened up the public domain to 160-acre tracts that were claimed, developed, and operated by family farmers.

The Morrill Act created the land grant college system with its network of agricultural research, experimentation, extension services, county agents, and the 4-H movement.

The Department of Agriculture began as a small government agency, but its operations have expanded enormously—especially in the past three decades. Today, its budget is second in size only to the Department of Defense.

What Mr. Khrushchev saw at the Garst farm was the culmination of a century of progress which had exploded into an agricultural revolution after World War II. He learned that the productivity of the American farmer for the past twenty years has moved ahead three times as swiftly as our industrial productivity. Indeed, the introduction of chemical fertilizers, hybrid seed, and pesticides, combined with mechanization, has wrought more spectacular increases in American agriculture in the last quarter century than in all our previous history.

Following his return to Russia, the Soviet leader stepped up his efforts to increase food production. He has repeatedly cajoled, scolded, admonished, and challenged Russian farmers to produce more wheat, corn, meat, and milk. The results to date have been disappointing and so Russia has joined Communist China in using precious foreign exchange to buy grain from the West, and the prospect is for additional purchases.

But one suspects that through continued and determined efforts Russia and China will solve their agricultural problems and become largely self-sufficient in food production. Both countries have an energetic people, vigorous government officials, and a determination to move ahead.

The crucial areas of world hunger today and in the future lie in Asia, Latin America, and Africa, in that order of urgency. These are the battlegrounds against hunger. These are the areas that need not only a growing volume of American food, but a widespread application of basic agricultural techniques developed years ago in the United States. I am confident that we hold the formula which can defeat hunger everywhere in the world.

If the developed nations will devote 10 percent of the resources and energy to the war against hunger that is now going into arms, there will be little real hunger in the world within a decade. We have the nuclear capacity to blow up the world without building one additional weapon. We have the agricultural capacity and knowledge to feed most of the world, without unreasonable sacrifice on our part.

For their part, the nations of Asia, Latin America, and Africa will have to concentrate their best efforts on strengthening agricultural production. They will need to double their food output by 1980 and triple it by 2000 if present population trends continue. Demographers predict that world population will double within thirty-five years, reaching a level of six billion by the year 2000. There is no reason to believe that population will multiply at that pace, however, if even minimum family planning practices can be developed. A rising standard of living and better nutrition seem to result in more interest in family planning. But even assuming the extreme population estimates prove to be right, this does not present an insoluble food problem.

The lines of attack on hunger must move out in two directions—an expanded distribution of farm surpluses in areas of food deficits, and the introduction of improved farming techniques to the developing world. The first approach is at best a temporary device but an invaluable one. The second approach is designed to end hunger permanently. Food for Peace can play an expanding role in both of these efforts. Our experience to date leaves no doubt that as we assist the development of other countries, they will be able to purchase larger quantities of food from us through normal commercial channels. Food for Peace should be viewed as a transition to normal marketing.

We are currently devoting about $2 billion annually

in farm commodities to Food for Peace. To wipe out
estimated food deficits for the current decade, we would
need to increase the program by $3 billion in food plus
another $1 billion to process, transport, and distribute
it. This total increase of $4 billion annually in food and
services would have to be supplemented by another
$1½ billion if by some turn of events we were to elim-
inate food deficits in mainland China. Thus, a total
additional investment of $5½ billion yearly, largely in
farm surpluses, would wipe out the food deficit worldwide for the current decade.

Although this is a large figure, it might prove to be
a reasonable cost for a better fed and possibly more
peaceful world. Much, if not all, of its true cost to the
nation would be recovered in improved income to
American agriculture and shipping, reduced storage
charges, and a general stimulus to U.S. income. If conditions permit us to reduce our present military budget
of $53 billion by 10 percent, we could underwrite this
expanded Food for Peace effort with no overall increase
in government spending.

It will probably require a similar annual investment
in funds, materials, and technical aid to win the other
more long-range line of attack on hunger—the moderni-
zation of the farm production in the developing world.
Fertilizer plants, pesticides, better seeds, simple farm
implements, and other farm aids, if applied on a major
scale designed to get substantial results in food output,
in this decade will add another $4 or $5 billion to the
war on hunger. A major part of this cost should be

financed by Western Europe, Japan, and Russia. With the United States underwriting a massive food distribution program, it is only right that the major financial cost of the overseas agricultural improvement program be financed by other countries.

The people of the United States, however, are best equipped to lead the effort for a better-fed world.

I would like, therefore, to suggest a ten-point battle plan against hunger led by the American people, which I am convinced will end in victory.

FIRST. We need a public recognition that our agricultural abundance is a valuable national asset that we intend to use increasingly to eliminate hunger from the world. I would like to hear the President of the United States and the Congress say that Food for Peace is a permanent, expanding program of the highest priority so long as there are large numbers of hungry human beings. We have urged our farmers to produce for war in the past; now let us ask them to enlist for the duration in the war against hunger. The Food for Peace legislative authority ought to be extended for at least five years at a time so that both American aid technicians and receiving governments can better integrate food assistance with development planning.

SECOND. We ought to establish a domestic farm policy based on production for human need rather than scarcity. Farm income must be protected—by direct cash payments if necessary. But we ought not to depend on severe cutbacks in production to maintain farm prices. There is something that goes against the moral grain when farmers drastically reduce food production and permit farms to be idled while others are hungry.

I was the principal author of a wheat bill that has been enacted into law for 1964 and 1965 that seeks a two-year voluntary reduction in wheat production. That would seem to be inconsistent with the philosophy of abundance just advanced. But control programs will be needed until such time as increases in our Food for Peace shipments have reduced our surplus stocks. Some kind of farm price or income stabilization device will doubtless be needed permanently. But I hope we will more and more orient our farm program around a vigorous effort to increase food uses overseas rather than restricting production at home.

By the end of this decade we ought to at least double the volume of Food for Peace distribution. To do that will call for greater, not less, U.S. production. Not to do so could mean major starvation in Latin America and Asia within a decade or less.

THIRD. I would like to see greater emphasis placed on nutritional standards in Food for Peace. The world's most serious food deficiency is the shortage of protein food, including meat, milk, eggs, soybean, and fish products. It is both more expensive and more difficult to move these commodities into overseas distribution than to ship surplus stocks of grain. But we can vastly improve the nutritional value of our school lunch programs and other food assistance if we substantially increase the protein portion.

Furthermore, the authority to purchase a broader range of protein foods such as beef and eggs would enable our government to strengthen our own agricultural economy. As this paragraph is being written, American livestock men have suffered a loss of billions of dollars because of declining beef prices. Yet, an expenditure of two or three hundred million dollars for the purchase of low-price cows could probably have prevented much of this disastrous loss to the American economy. And it would have added urgently needed protein to Food for Peace. The same double argument can be made for eggs and poultry and other produce. Indeed, there is a third argument for broadening the content of the Food for Peace package. Children who learn to eat hamburger and chicken and eggs today will build the kind of healthy bodies and appetites that will enable them to be cash customers tomorrow. No better proof of this can be found than the remarkable transition of Japan from Food for Peace recipient to Uncle Sam's best agricultural customer.

There would be some minor problems of processing and preserving meats and other protein foods but our scientists and technicians could quickly solve those problems. They are not nearly so difficult or as expensive to solve as the development of a jet engine or a Polaris submarine.

FOURTH. I believe that we should eliminate the political restrictions on our Food for Peace program. Various legislative and administrative rulings now prevent us from selling or granting food to most of the people who are so unfortunate as to live under Communist governments. I think this is a mistake which deprives us of a unique opportunity to advance our national interest and the peace of the world.

St. Paul admonished "If thine enemy hunger, feed him." Applied to Food for Peace that advice is not only good religion; it is good economics and good politics.

It is good religion because it builds on the assumption that all men are brothers—even those who disagree.

It is good economics because it recognizes that a billion people live in the Communist world and that breaking down the barriers to international commerce in nonstrategic materials can be of material benefit to all.

It is good politics because it enables us to demonstrate the superiority of free, independent, family-type agriculture over the collectivized farms of the Communist world. In time this could lead to an important modification of the Communist system.

Food is one of the common denominators of international life. It ought not to be used as a barrier to divide mankind; it should serve as a unifying force in the world.

It is especially important that we remove political restrictions on our child-feeding programs. The cold war has claimed enough victims without applying it to infants, nursing mothers, and school children.

Of course, removing the political barriers around Food for Peace might not prompt all foreign governments, including mainland China, to admit U.S. food. But at least we would have taken a positive position before the world that will enhance both our moral and political capacity as a great power.

I think the American people overwhelmingly favored the commercial sale of wheat to the Soviet Union in 1963. I am equally convinced that they would support a policy of feeding hungry people in China or Cuba or any other country in spite of our dislike for their government. When I was Director of Food for Peace in 1961, our office received literally thousands of letters from Americans in every walk of life urging that we offer food to relieve the famine on the Chinese mainland. No other issue drew so much spontaneous mail and so many thoughtfully written letters.

One tough-minded veteran Congressman suggested early in 1961 that the President publicly inform the Chinese that American ships loaded with wheat were on the way. They would be welcome to the wheat provided the Red Cross were permitted to supervise its distribution. If they rejected it, the ships would head for Hong Kong and the wheat would be stored there for the refugees. I still think this was an experiment worth trying.

In short, I regard our food abundance as a blessing of the Lord that ought to be taken out of the context of the cold war.

FIFTH. I would recommend an international pre-school and school lunch program aimed at every needy child in the world. There are approximately a billion children in the world under the age of fifteen. At least half of them are suffering from malnutrition. Food for

Peace school lunches are reaching forty million of these. Another fifteen million preschool age children are also benefitting from the program. A minority of the neediest youngsters are enrolled in school; others will be difficult to reach. But hungry children have a way of seeking out a school where food is served. In this way school lunches generate both nutrition and education! A sustained effort can bring at least one nutritious meal a day to most of the world's half a billion needy youngsters. We can make no greater contribution to the physical, mental, and spiritual health of mankind.

SIXTH. We can at least triple the number of food-for-wages projects in the developing world. A much greater use can be made of our agricultural abundance as a tool to finance a major portion of thousands of new community and rural development efforts of all kinds.

SEVENTH. A substantial portion of the foreign currencies generated by Food for Peace sales plus some of our foreign aid funds should be used to improve facilities for handling and distributing our food abroad. There is an urgent need for improved port facilities, storage, and internal transport. Some of the currencies should also be used to purchase utensils, implements, and other items designed to strengthen the institutional feeding and economic development programs of our voluntary agencies.

EIGHTH. Peace Corps volunteers should be more widely enlisted in the Food for Peace effort. American volunteers are needed as supervisors on food-for-work and school lunch projects. They are needed as nutri-

tionists and as assistants in the handling and preparation of food. They are needed most of all in sharing
American agricultural know-how with the farmers of
the developing world.

In addition, private industry experts, researchers, and
technicians are needed—men and women who will take
leave of their jobs for a period of time to share their
knowledge of food handling, nutrition, or agriculture
with our friends abroad.

NINTH. We need to weight our foreign aid program more sharply on the side of agricultural development. We should never forget that eight out of ten
human beings on this planet make their living on the
land. Furthermore, few if any countries can advance
industrially before they have achieved a sound agricultural base.

Too much of our foreign aid has gone to sophisticated
industrial development prematurely. We need to concentrate much more on the introduction of improved
farming methods—irrigataion, fertilizer, pesticides, hybrid seeds, and other tested devices. These methods
can break the chronic cycle of underproduction, hunger,
and poverty in a world which is still largely rural.

America has an invaluable reservoir of trained extension workers, county agents, and land-grant college
graduates. Many more such trained men and women
are needed overseas. Some of our farm-related industries such as fertilizer manufacturers could loan some
of their technicians for service overseas.

There are thousands of retired farmers who could

give a year's service abroad to assist in the operation of American-run demonstration farms. Heavy farm machinery is not needed in Asia, Latin America, and Africa, where the labor supply is so enormous. What is needed are simple techniques and tested devices such as chemical fertilizers that have multiplied the production of American agriculture several times over in recent decades.

TENTH. America should continue and expand its role in the multilateral Freedom from Hunger Campaign and other international efforts. Such distinguished and highly successful development experts as Paul Hoffman, Director of the United Nations Special Fund, and Eugene Black, former director of the World Bank, are firmly convinced that a large percentage of our aid should be funneled through international agencies. This device removes the suspicion of economic imperialism and the manipulation of other people's national affairs. It also relieves us of the burden of establishing and enforcing fair criteria for self-help aid programs. It is easier for an international agency to insist on definite performance standards by recipients of aid than it is for a rich neighbor seeking political favor to do so.

I am fully convinced that these ten steps represent a nearly certain answer to the challenge of hunger. They seek to build on the remarkable success which Food for Peace has already achieved.

Recently, one of our church-affiliated conferences issued a poignant statement observing that "there are those who do not have enough to eat. Their clothing is worn and threadbare. They are overcrowded in wretched housing. They have no privacy, not even the mercy of silence. And, the greatest hurt of all, they feel rejected and unwanted. They could die, and no one would shed a tear."

Food for Peace is not the only answer to that touching challenge, but it speaks with a generous heart and offers a warm hand to a hungry humanity. It is, indeed, a major weapon in America's war against want.

APPENDIX I

The Food for Peace Program

U.S. TOTAL ECONOMIC ASSISTANCE EFFORT
FISCAL YEAR 1963
(IN MILLIONS)

FOOD FOR PEACE 34% $1,777

A.I.D. CAPITAL INVESTMENT AND TECHNICAL ASSISTANCE 46% $2,396

EXPORT IMPORT BANK 11% $572

OTHER 9% $438

PEACE CORPS
SOCIAL PROGRESS TRUST FUND
SUBSCRIPTIONS TO INTER-AMERICAN DEVELOPMENT
                    INTERNATIONAL DEVELOPMENT ASSOCIATION
UN BONDS

The Main Categories of
Food for Peace Operations

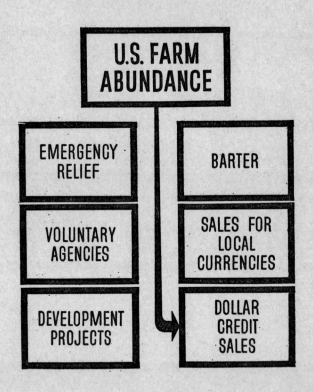

U.S. FARM
ABUNDANCE

EMERGENCY
RELIEF

BARTER

VOLUNTARY
AGENCIES

SALES FOR
LOCAL
CURRENCIES

DEVELOPMENT
PROJECTS

DOLLAR
CREDIT
SALES

THE FOOD FOR PEACE PROGRAM
(Fiscal Year 1963)

	Amounts Programed (millions)	People (millions)	Countries 1963 (55-63)	Title
Sales (76%)				
Local currency	$1,226		27 (46)	I
Dollar credit	82		9 (15)	IV
Barter	38		30 (108)	III
	$1,346			
	(Figures converted to market value for comparative purposes)			
Donations (24%)				
Voluntary agencies	$260	77	115 (133)	III
Disaster relief	120	16	16 (58)	II
Self-help projects	51	7	19 (25)	II
	431	100		
	$1,777			

Food For Peace
Shipments – World Regions

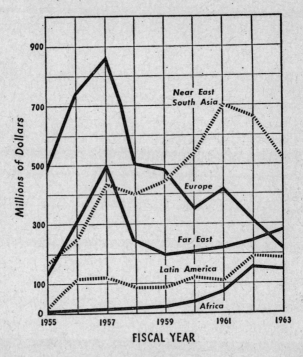

Millions of Dollars

Near East
South Asia

Europe

Far East

Latin America

Africa

FISCAL YEAR

1955   1957   1959   1961   1963

900

700

500

300

100

0

APPENDIX II

A Partial List of Voluntary Participants in the Food for Peace Program

THE AMERICAN FOOD FOR PEACE COUNCIL

EXECUTIVE COMMITTEE

Chairman: MR. PAUL S. WILLIS
President, Grocery Manufacturers of America, Inc.

Executive Secretary: MR. HARRY LeBOVIT

MR. C. G. ADAMY *
Executive Vice President
National Association of Food
  Chains

MR. DWAYNE O. ANDREAS *
Executive Vice President
Farmers Union Grain Terminal
  Association

MR. CLARK M. CLIFFORD *
Clifford and Miller
Attorneys and Counsellors at
  Law

MR. ALED P. DAVIES
Vice President
American Meat Institute

MR. GEORGE M. ELSEY *

MR. HUGH FARLEY *
Chairman
American Council of Voluntary
  Agencies for Foreign Service

MR. E. LEE FELLER *
President
Fellmen Associates, Inc.

MR. CLIFFORD R. HOPE *

DR. ROY M. KOTTMAN
American Association of Land-
  Grant Colleges and State
  Universities

* Private citizen—not representing an organization.

135

Mr. Murray D. Lincoln *
President
Nationwide Mutual Insurance
   Co.

Mr. A. N. McFarlane *
Executive Officer
Corn Products Company

Mrs. Florence S. Mahoney *
Cox Newspapers

Mr. Joe Mooney *
Senior Vice President
American Sugar Company

Mr. Robert Nathan *
President
Robert Nathan Associates

Mr. Herschel D. Newsom
Master
The National Grange

Mr. James G. Patton
President
National Farmers Union

Dr. John Perryman
Executive Director
American School Food Service
   Assn.

Mr. L. C. Roll *
President
Kellogg Company

Mr. Arthur Rosenstock
President
American Newspaper Guild

Mr. Alvin Shapiro
Vice President
American Merchant Marine
   Institute

Mr. Charles B. Shuman
President
American Farm Bureau
   Federation

Mr. A. B. Sparboe
Chamber of Commerce of the
   United States

Mr. Jesse Tapp
Chairman of the Board of
   Directors
Bank of America

Mr. George W. Weigold
Managing Director
Dairy Society International

Mr. Frank K. White
The Advertising Council, Inc.

Mr. R. D. Wooster *
Executive Vice President
The Borden Company

* Private citizen—not representing an organization.

THE AMERICAN FREEDOM FROM HUNGER FOUNDATION, INC.

OFFICERS

HONORABLE HARRY S. TRUMAN
Independence, Missouri
  (Honorary Chairman)

MR. THOMAS M. WARE
President and Director
International Minerals and
  Chemical Corporation
Skokie, Illinois
  (Chairman of the Board)

MR. HERBERT J. SUGDEN
Washington, D.C.
  (President)

MR. ROBERT R. NATHAN
Washington, D.C.
  (First Vice President)

MR. JOSEPH MCGARRY
Vice President
International Minerals and
  Chemical Corporation
Skokie, Illinois
  (Vice President)

MR. DOUGLAS R. SMITH,
  President
National Savings & Trust
  Company
Washington, D.C.
  (Treasurer)

MR. JAMES J. O'CONNOR
Executive Director
The Academy of Food
  Marketing
St. Joseph's College
Philadelphia, Pennsylvania
  (Secretary)

MR. RICHARD SCHIFTER
Washington, D.C.
  (Legal Counsel)

MR. ARTHUR C. RINGLAND
Chevy Chase, Maryland
  (Historian)

EXECUTIVE COMMITTEE

Mr. Homer Brinkley
Falls Church, Virginia

Dr. Philip V. Cardon
Washington, D.C.

Dr. Russell Coleman,
President
The Sulphur Institute
Washington, D.C.

Mr. Aled P. Davies,
Vice President
American Meat Institute
Chicago, Illinois

Mr. Harry Edell
Washington, D.C.

Mrs. Orville L. Freeman
Washington, D.C.

Mr. Tom Gill, President
International Society of
Tropical Foresters
Washington, D.C.

Honorable George
McGovern
United States Senator
Mitchell, South Dakota

Dr. Herschel Newsom,
Master
The National Grange
Washington, D.C.

Mr. James G. Patton,
President
National Farmers Union
Washington, D.C.

Mr. Walter P. Reuther,
President
International Union, UAW
Detroit, Michigan

Mr. Alvin Shapiro,
Vice President
American Merchant Marine
Institute, Inc.
Washington, D.C.

The Most Reverend
Edward E. Swanstrom
Executive Director
Catholic Relief Services
New York, New York

Dr. Howard M. Teaf, Jr.
Haverford, Pennsylvania

Mr. Harold A. Vogel,
Director
North American Regional
Office
Food and Agriculture
Organization
Washington, D.C.

Dr. LeRoy Voris,
Executive Director
Food and Nutrition Board
National Academy of Sciences
Washington, D.C.

Mr. Paul S. Willis, President
Grocery Manufacturers of
America
New York, New York

BOARD OF TRUSTEES

MR. CLYDE ELLIS,
General Manager
National Rural Electric
Cooperative Association
Washington, D.C.

DR. NOVICE G. FAWCETT,
President
Ohio State University
Columbus, Ohio

MRS. ORVILLE L. FREEMAN
Washington, D.C.

MR. THOMAS GILL, President
International Society of
Tropical Foresters
Washington, D.C.

DR. GRACE GOLDSMITH,
Chairman
Food and Nutrition Board
Tulane University
New Orleans, Louisiana

MR. J. PETER GRACE, President
W. R. Grace and Company
New York, New York

MR. FOWLER HAMILTON
New York, New York

MRS. VANCE HARTKE
Washington, D.C.

MR. FREDERICK W. HATCH
Monsanto Chemical Company
New York, New York

MR. FRED HEINKEL, President
Missouri Farmers Association
Columbia, Missouri

MRS. CHARLES HYMES
Minneapolis, Minnesota

HONORABLE MARVIN JONES
Chief Judge
U.S. Court of Claims
Washington, D.C.

MR. BURTON JOSEPH, President
I. S. Joseph Company, Inc.
Minneapolis, Minnesota

MR. EDGAR F. KAISER,
President
Kaiser Industries Corporation
Oakland, California

MR. GEORGE KILLION,
President
American President Lines, Ltd.
San Francisco, California

DR. FLEMMIE P. KITTRELL
Dean, School of Home
Economics
Howard University
Washington, D.C.

DR. RALPH E. LAPP
Nuclear Physicist
Washington, D.C.

MRS. ALBERT D. LASKER
New York, New York

MR. MURRAY D. LINCOLN,
President
Nationwide Mutual Insurance
Company
Columbus, Ohio

MR. F. P. LONGEWAY, JR.
National Fisheries Institute
Washington, D.C.

REV. HENRY A. McCANNA
Executive Director
Department of Town and
   Country Church
New York, New York

MR. JOSEPH M. McGARRY
Vice President
International Minerals and
   Chemical Corporation
Skokie, Illinois

HONORABLE GEORGE
   McGOVERN
United States Senator
Mitchell, South Dakota

MR. ROBERT D. McMILLEN
Corn Industries Research
   Foundation, Inc.
Washington, D.C.

HONORABLE GEORGE MEANY
President, AFL-CIO
Washington, D.C.

DR. RAYMOND W. MILLER
Public Relations Research
   Associates, Inc.
Washington, D.C.

MR. ROBERT R. NATHAN
Washington, D.C.

DR. HERSCHEL NEWSOM,
   Master
The National Grange
Washington, D.C.

MR. JAMES J. O'CONNOR
Executive Director
The Academy of Food
   Marketing

St. Joseph's College
Philadelphia, Pennsylvania

DR. FREDERICK D. PATTERSON,
   President
Phelps Stokes Fund
New York, New York

MR. JAMES G. PATTON,
   President
National Farmers Union
Washington, D.C.

MR. WALTER P. REUTHER,
   President
International Union, UAW
Detroit, Michigan

MR. J. LOUIS REYNOLDS
Chairman of the Board
Reynolds International
Richmond, Virginia

MR. ARTHUR C. RINGLAND
Chevy Chase, Maryland

MR. DAVID SARNOFF
Chairman of the Board
Radio Corporation of America
New York, New York

MR. RICHARD SCHIFTER,
   Attorney
Washington, D.C.

MR. ALVIN SHAPIRO,
   Vice President
American Merchant Marine
   Institute
Washington, D.C.

MR. DOUGLAS R. SMITH,
   President

National Savings and Trust
Company
Washington, D.C.

Mr. H. Christian Sonne,
President
National Planning Association
New York, New York

Dr. Asa T. Spaulding
North Carolina Mutual Life
Insurance Company
Durham, North Carolina

Mr. Lionel Steinberg,
Vice President
California State Board of
Agriculture
Thermal, California

Honorable Adlai E. Stevenson
U.S. Ambassador to the United
Nations
New York, New York

Mr. Herbert J. Sugden,
President
American Freedom from
Hunger Foundation
Washington, D.C.

Mr. Arthur Hays Sulzberger
Chairman of the Board
The New York Times
New York, New York

The Most Reverend
Edward E. Swanstrom
Executive Director
Catholic Relief Services
New York, New York

Mr. Charles P. Taft
Cincinnati, Ohio

Dr. Howard M. Teaf, Jr.
Haverford College
Haverford, Pennsylvania

Mr. Charles Tyroler, II
Counselors on National
Problems
Washington, D.C.

Mr. Harold A. Vogel,
Director
North American Regional
Office
Food and Agriculture
Organization
Washington, D.C.

Dr. LeRoy Voris,
Executive Director
Food and Nutrition Board
National Academy of Sciences
Washington, D.C.

Mr. Thomas M. Ware
President and Director
International Minerals and
Chemical Corporation
Skokie, Illinois

Dr. Oliver S. Willham,
President
Oklahoma State University
Stillwater, Oklahoma

Mr. Paul S. Willis, President
Grocery Manufacturers of
America
New York, New York

Mrs. Arthur L. Zepf,
Past President
National Council of Catholic
Women
Toledo, Ohio

AMERICAN COUNCIL OF VOLUNTARY AGENCIES FOR FOREIGN SERVICE, INC.

MEMBER AGENCIES

American Baptist Relief

American Council for Judaism Philanthropic Fund, Inc.

American Friends of Russian Freedom, Inc.

American Friends Service Committee, Inc.

American Fund for Czechoslovak Refugees, Inc.

American Jewish Joint Distribution Committee, Inc.

American Leprosy Missions, Inc.

American Middle East Rehabilitation, Inc.

American National Committee to Aid Homeless Armenians (ANCHA)

American ORT Federation, Inc.

American Relief for Poland, Inc.

Assemblies of God—Foreign Missions Department, General Council of the Brethren Service Commission

CARE, Inc.

Catholic Relief Services—National Catholic Welfare Conference, Inc.

Church World Service, Inc., National Council of the Churches of Christ in the U.S.A.

Co-ordinated Hungarian Relief, Inc.

Hadassah, The Women's Zionist Org. of America, Inc.

Hadassah Medical Relief Association, Inc.

Heifer Project, Inc.

International Rescue Committee, Inc.

Iran Foundation, Inc.

Lutheran Immigration Service, National Lutheran Council—Lutheran Church—Missouri Synod

Lutheran World Relief, Inc.

Mennonite Central Committee, Inc.

Near East Foundation

Polish American Immigration and Relief Committee, Inc.

Salvation Army, The

Seventh-Day Adventist Welfare Service, Inc.

Tolstoy Foundation, Inc.

Unitarian Universalist Service Committee, Inc.

United Friends of Needy and Displaced People of Yugoslavia, Inc.

United Hias Service, Inc.

United Lithuanian Relief Fund of America, Inc.

United Seamen's Service, Inc.

United Ukrainian American Relief Committee, Inc.

World Relief Commission of the National Association of Evangelicals

World University Service

Young Women's Christian Association of the U.S.A. (International Division)

UNITED STATES TRADE GROUPS COOPERATING IN FOREIGN MARKET DEVELOPMENT

Cotton Council International
Memphis, Tennessee
    William Rhea Blake, Executive Vice President and Secretary
Soybean Council of America, Inc.
Waterloo, Iowa
    Howard L. Roach, President
American Soybean Association
Hudson, Iowa
    George M. Strayer, Executive Vice President
    Howard E. Grow, Assistant to Executive Vice President
Institute of American Poultry Industries
Chicago, Illinois
    Harold M. Williams, President
Dairy Society International
Washington, D.C.
    George W. Weigold, Managing Director
The American Jersey Cattle Club
Columbus, Ohio
    James F. Cavanaugh, Executive Secretary
Holstein-Freisian Association of America
Brattleboro, Vermont
    Robert H. Rumler, Executive Secretary
Brown Swiss Cattle Breeders' Association
Beloit, Wisconsin
    Marvin L. Kruse, Secretary

The American Guernsey Cattle Club
Peterborough, New Hampshire
    Robert D. Stewart, Secretary

Ayrshire Breeder's Association
Brandon, Vermont
    David Gibson, Jr., Executive Secretary

Purebred Dairy Cattle Association
Peterborough, New Hampshire
    Karl B. Musser, Secretary

American Dry Milk Institute, Inc.
Chicago, Illinois
    John T. Walsh, Executive Director

California Prune Advisory Board
San Francisco, California
    Ray W. Jewell, Manager

Florida Citrus Commission
Lakeland, Florida
    Frank Arn, Director, Merchandising and Advertising

California-Arizona Citrus League
Los Angeles, California
    Russell Z. Eller, Coordinator

The Cranberry Institute
South Duxbury, Massachusetts
    Orrin G. Colley, President

Red Cherry Exports, Inc.
Grand Rapids, Michigan
    Berkeley I. Freeman, Secretary-Manager

California Raisin Advisory Board
Fresno, California
    Donald C. White, Manager

Dried Fruit Association of California
San Jose, California
    Al E. Thorpe, Executive Vice President

National Canners Association
Washington, D.C.
    Milan Smith, Executive Vice President
    Leonard Lobred, Director

Northwest Horticultural Council
Yakima, Washington
    Ernest Falk, Manager

Great Plains Wheat, Inc.
Garden City, Kansas
    Howard W. Hardy, President

Western Wheat Associates, U.S.A., Inc.
Portland, Oregon
    Richard K. Baum, Executive Vice President

Millers' National Federation
Washington, D.C.
    Gordon Boals, Director, Export Programs

U.S. Feed Grains Council
Washington, D.C.
    Clarence D. Palmby, Executive Vice President

U.S. Rice, Inc.
Ganado, Texas
    Marcus W. Mauritz, President

National Dry Bean Council
Washington, D.C.
    Harold Lovre, Secretary

American Seed Trade Association
Washington, D.C.
    William Heckendorn, Executive Secretary

American Brahman Breeders' Association
Houston, Texas
    Harry P. Gayden, Executive Secretary

National Renderers Association
Chicago, Illinois
    Dean A. Specht, Executive Director

Western States Meat Packers Association, Inc.
Washington, D.C.
    L. Blaine Liljenquist, President and General Manager

American Angus Association
St. Joseph, Missouri
    Glen S. Bratcher, Secretary

Tanners' Council of America, Inc.
New York, New York
    Irving R. Glass, Executive Vice President

American Hereford Association
Kansas City, Missouri
    Paul Swaffar, Secretary

International Brangus Breeders Association
Kansas City, Missouri
    Jesse L. Dowdy, Secretary

United Duroc Swine Registry
Peoria, Illinois
    R. E. Judd, Secretary

Poland China Record Association
Galesburg, Illinois
    Claude W. Mitchell, Secretary

National Livestock & Meat Board
Chicago, Illinois
    Carl F. Newmann, Secretary and General Manager

Santa Gertrudis Breeders International
Kingsville, Texas
    R. P. Marshall, Executive Secretary

Tobacco Associates, Inc.
Washington, D.C.
    J. B. Hutson, President
    J. C. Frink, Vice President

Leaf Tobacco Exporters Association, Inc.
Raleigh, North Carolina
    Malcolm B. Seawell, Executive Secretary

Burley & Dark Leaf Tobacco Export Association, Inc.
Washington, D.C.
    Frank B. Snodgrass, Vice President and Managing Director

Virginia Dark-Fired and Sun-Cured Tobacco Export Association,
    Inc.
Farmville, Virginia
    E. P. Lancaster, Executive Vice President and General
    Manager